The Latest Mediterranean

Air Fryer Cookbook

A Wealth of Amazing Delicious, Super Easy Recipes for Living Well and Eating Well Every Day with Stress-Free 30-Day Meal Plan |With Full-Color Images

Jennifer B. Green

TABLE OF CONTENTS

120 Mediterranean Recipes for Air Fryers

Embark on a culinary voyage through the enchanting flavors of the Mediterranean with our innovative collection of air fryer recipes! Delve into the tantalizing aromas and bold tastes inspired by the azure waters and sun-kissed landscapes of this vibrant region. From zesty lemon-infused seafood to aromatic herb-packed meats, experience the magic of Mediterranean cuisine reinvented for the modern kitchen. Each recipe is crafted to bring out the essence of Mediterranean cooking while embracing the convenience and health benefits of air frying. Whether you're savoring the tangy spices of Turkey, the rustic simplicity of Spain, or the vibrant freshness of Provence, these recipes promise a culinary adventure that's both delicious and nutritious. Prepare to elevate your cooking game and delight your senses with every bite!

What is the Mediterranean Diet?

The Mediterranean Diet is not just a way of eating; it's a lifestyle celebrated for its health benefits and cultural richness. Rooted in the culinary traditions

of countries bordering the Mediterranean Sea, this diet emphasizes whole, minimally processed foods, abundant in fruits, vegetables, whole grains, legumes, nuts, and olive oil. It also includes moderate amounts of fish, poultry, and dairy, with limited consumption of red meat and sweets.

What sets the Mediterranean Diet apart is its emphasis on balance and diversity. Meals are typically shared with family and friends, fostering a sense of community and enjoyment. The diet is not only delicious but also renowned for its numerous health benefits, including reduced risk of heart disease, stroke, and certain cancers. The Mediterranean lifestyle extends beyond food, encompassing regular physical activity, mindful eating, and a relaxed approach to life.

In essence, the Mediterranean Diet isn't just about what you eat—it's about embracing a holistic approach to wellness that nourishes both body and soul.

Health Benefits of Mediterranean Diet

The Mediterranean Diet isn't just a flavorful culinary experience; it's also renowned for its numerous health benefits, supported by extensive research and centuries of cultural practice.

1. Heart Health: One of the most well-documented benefits of the Mediterranean Diet is its positive impact on heart health. The abundance of heart-healthy fats from olive oil, nuts, and fatty fish, coupled with the low consumption of saturated fats from red meat, helps lower LDL cholesterol levels and reduce the risk of heart disease.

2. Reduced Inflammation: Rich in fruits, vegetables, whole grains, and olive oil, the Mediterranean Diet is packed with antioxidants and anti-inflammatory properties. These nutrients help combat oxidative stress and reduce inflammation in the body, which is linked to chronic diseases like cancer, arthritis, and Alzheimer's.

3. Weight Management: Despite its emphasis on indulgent flavors, the Mediterranean Diet is associated with weight management and lower rates of obesity. The focus on whole, nutrient-dense foods and portion control promotes satiety and helps

maintain a healthy weight over the long term.

4. Improved Cognitive Function: Studies suggest that adhering to the Mediterranean Diet may support brain health and reduce the risk of cognitive decline as you age. The combination of omega-3 fatty acids from fish, antioxidants from fruits and vegetables, and polyphenols from olive oil may help protect against neurodegenerative diseases like Alzheimer's.

5. Diabetes Prevention: The Mediterranean Diet's emphasis on complex carbohydrates, such as whole grains and legumes, along with its moderate consumption of healthy fats and lean proteins, can help stabilize blood sugar levels and improve insulin sensitivity. This makes it an effective dietary approach for preventing and managing type 2 diabetes.

In summary, the Mediterranean Diet offers a delicious and sustainable way of eating that not only tantalizes the taste buds but also nourishes the body and promotes overall well-being.

How to Use an Air Fryer

Unlock the culinary magic of your air fryer with these simple yet effective tips:

1. Preheat: Just like with a conventional oven, preheating your air fryer ensures that your food cooks evenly and crisps up perfectly. Most air fryers require only a few minutes to preheat, so don't skip this step for optimal results.

2. Lightly Oil: While air fryers are known for their ability to cook with little to no oil, a light spritz or brush of oil can enhance the crispiness and flavor of your dishes. Opt for heart-healthy oils like olive, avocado, or coconut oil, and use them sparingly to keep your recipes light and nutritious.

3. Arrange Food Evenly: To ensure uniform cooking, arrange your food in a single layer inside the air fryer basket, making sure not to overcrowd it. This allows hot air to circulate evenly around each piece, resulting in crispier and more evenly cooked meals.

4. Shake or Flip: Midway through the cooking process, pause to shake or flip your food for even browning and crisping on all sides. Use tongs or a spatula to gently move the food around in the basket, then resume cooking to perfection.

5. Monitor Temperature and Time: Keep an eye on the cooking temperature and time to prevent overcooking or burning. Most air fryer recipes provide recommended cooking temperatures and times, but you may need to adjust based on your specific model and preferences.

6. Experiment with Seasonings: Get creative with your seasonings and flavorings to customize your air-fried creations. From herbs and spices to marinades and sauces, the possibilities are endless. Just be mindful of adding wet ingredients, as they can affect the crispiness of your food.

7. Clean Regularly: To maintain optimal performance and prevent lingering flavors from previous meals, clean your air fryer regularly according to the manufacturer's instructions. Most parts are dishwasher safe or can be easily cleaned with warm, soapy water.

By following these tips, you'll be well on your way to mastering the art of air frying and enjoying delicious, crispy meals with ease.

Why Use an Air Fryer for Mediterranean Cuisine

Using an air fryer to prepare Mediterranean cuisine offers a plethora of benefits, perfectly complementing the flavors and cooking techniques inherent to this vibrant culinary tradition. Here's why incorporating an air fryer into your Mediterranean cooking repertoire can take your dishes to the next level:

1. Healthier Cooking: The Mediterranean Diet emphasizes fresh, wholesome ingredients and minimal processing, making it inherently healthy. Air frying aligns perfectly with this ethos by allowing you to achieve that crispy texture you crave with significantly less oil than traditional frying methods.

By using hot air circulation to cook food, air fryers can reduce the amount of unhealthy fats and calories in your meals while preserving their delicious taste.

2. Retained Nutrients: Air frying preserves the nutritional integrity of ingredients, allowing you to reap the full benefits of the Mediterranean Diet's nutrient-rich foods. Unlike deep frying, which can strip foods of their vitamins and minerals, air frying locks in essential nutrients, ensuring that your dishes are as nutritious as they are delicious.

3. Enhanced Flavors: Air frying provides a unique cooking method that results in beautifully caramelized exteriors and tender interiors, intensifying the natural flavors of Mediterranean ingredients. Whether you're air frying vegetables, seafood, or meats, you'll find that the crispiness achieved enhances the taste and texture of your dishes, elevating them to gourmet status.

4. Time and Energy Efficiency: Air fryers offer a convenient way to cook Mediterranean-inspired meals without the need for extensive prep or cleanup. With rapid cooking times and minimal preheating required, you can whip up your favorite dishes in a fraction of the time it would take using traditional methods. Plus, air fryers typically consume less energy than conventional ovens, making them an eco-friendly choice for busy home cooks.

5. Versatility: From crispy falafel to golden-brown spanakopita, air fryers can handle a wide range of Mediterranean recipes with ease. Their versatility allows you to experiment with different ingredients and cooking techniques, from frying and roasting to baking and grilling, all in one compact appliance. Whether you're cooking for a weeknight dinner or entertaining guests, an air fryer offers endless possibilities for delicious Mediterranean-inspired creations.

In summary, using an air fryer for Mediterranean cuisine combines the health-conscious principles of the Mediterranean Diet with the convenience and versatility of modern cooking technology. By harnessing the power of hot air circulation, you can achieve crispy, flavorful results that are sure to delight your taste buds while nourishing your body with the wholesome goodness of Mediterranean ingredients.

Menu Planning for a Mediterranean Air Fryer Meal

Crafting a Mediterranean-inspired meal with your air fryer offers endless possibilities for a flavorful and wholesome dining experience. Here's how to plan a menu that celebrates the vibrant flavors and fresh ingredients of the Mediterranean:

Appetizers:

● Crispy Zucchini Fritters: Grate zucchini and mix with garlic, feta cheese, and fresh herbs before air frying until golden and crispy. Serve with a side of tzatziki sauce for dipping.

● Stuffed Bell Peppers: Fill halved bell peppers with a mixture of quinoa, cherry tomatoes, olives, and feta cheese, then air fry until tender and slightly charred.

Main Course:

● Mediterranean Chicken Shawarma: Marinate chicken thighs in a blend of yogurt, lemon juice, and spices, then air fry until juicy and flavorful. Serve with warm pita bread, hummus, and a side of tabbouleh salad.

● Crispy Eggplant Caprese: Layer slices of eggplant with fresh mozzarella, tomatoes, and basil, then air fry until golden and bubbling. Drizzle with balsamic glaze before serving for an extra burst of flavor.

Sides:

● Greek-Style Roasted Potatoes: Toss potato wedges with olive oil, garlic, lemon zest, and oregano, then air fry until crispy and golden brown. These flavorful potatoes are the perfect accompaniment to any Mediterranean meal.

● Mediterranean Quinoa Salad: Combine cooked quinoa with diced cucumber, cherry tomatoes, Kalamata olives, red onion, and crumbled feta cheese. Dress with a lemon-herb vinaigrette for a light and refreshing side dish.

Dessert:

● Honey Roasted Peach Sundaes: Halve peaches and remove the pits, then drizzle with honey and sprinkle with cinnamon before air frying until caramelized and tender. Serve with a scoop of vanilla ice cream and a sprinkle of toasted almonds for an indulgent yet light dessert.

Beverage:

● Watermelon Mint Agua Fresca: Blend fresh watermelon with a handful of mint leaves and a squeeze of lime juice, then strain and serve over ice for a refreshing and hydrating beverage that's perfect for sipping on a warm day.

With this diverse and flavorful menu, you can create a Mediterranean-inspired feast that's sure to impress your guests and transport them to the sun-drenched shores of the Mediterranean. Enjoy the delicious flavors and wholesome ingredients that this vibrant cuisine has to offer!

About the Recipes

In our recipe collection, we've carefully curated a selection of dishes that marry the health-conscious principles of the Mediterranean diet with the convenience and innovation of air frying. Here's what makes our recipes stand out:

1. Wholesome Ingredients: Every recipe features wholesome, nutrient-rich ingredients that are central to the Mediterranean diet. From vibrant vegetables and lean proteins to heart-healthy fats and whole grains, our recipes prioritize fresh, unprocessed foods that promote overall well-being.

2. Mediterranean Influence: Inspired by the flavors and traditions of the Mediterranean region, our recipes capture the essence of this celebrated cuisine. Whether it's the aromatic spices of Morocco, the sun-kissed flavors of Greece, or the rustic simplicity of Italy, each dish pays homage to the diverse and vibrant culinary heritage of the Mediterranean.

3. Air Fryer Innovation: By harnessing the power of hot air circulation, our recipes demonstrate how the air fryer can achieve the crispy textures and delicious flavors of traditional Mediterranean dishes with minimal oil and fuss. From golden-brown falafel to perfectly roasted vegetables, the air fryer offers a healthier and more convenient way to enjoy your favorite Mediterranean flavors.

4. Health-Conscious Cooking: With air frying, you can indulge in the irresistible taste of fried foods without the guilt. Our recipes use little to no oil, resulting in lighter, lower-calorie versions of classic Mediterranean dishes. Plus, air frying helps retain the natural nutrients and flavors of the ingredients, ensuring that each dish is as nutritious as it is delicious.

5. Variety and Versatility: Whether you're in the mood for appetizers, main courses, sides, or desserts, our recipe collection has you covered. From quick and easy weeknight meals to impressive dishes for special occasions, you'll find a diverse array of Mediterranean-inspired recipes that are simple to prepare and bursting with flavor.

In essence, our recipes offer a delicious and convenient way to embrace the healthful and flavorful traditions of the Mediterranean diet using the innovative cooking technology of the air fryer. With our collection, you can enjoy the best of both worlds—wholesome, Mediterranean-inspired dishes that are as good for your body as they are for your taste buds.

Chapter 1: Breakfast Recipes

Homemade Gluten-Free Granola Cereal

Prep time: 7 minutes / Cook time: 30 minutes / Makes 3½ cups

Ingredients:
• Oil spray
• 1½ cups (150g) gluten-free rolled oats
• 1/2 cup (60g) walnuts, chopped
• 1/2 cup (60g) almonds, chopped
• 1/2 cup (65g) pumpkin seeds
• 1/4 cup (85g) maple syrup or honey
• 1 tablespoon toasted sesame oil or vegetable oil
• 1 teaspoon ground cinnamon
• 1/2 teaspoon salt
• 1/2 cup (60g) dried cranberries

Instructions:
1. Preheat the air fryer to 250ºF (121ºC). Line the air fryer basket with parchment paper and lightly spray with oil.
2. In a large bowl, combine the gluten-free rolled oats, walnuts, almonds, pumpkin seeds, maple syrup or honey, toasted sesame oil or vegetable oil, ground cinnamon, and salt.
3. Spread the mixture evenly in the prepared basket.
4. Cook for 30 minutes, stirring every 10 minutes to ensure even cooking.
5. Transfer the granola to a bowl, add the dried cranberries, and mix well.
6. Allow the granola to cool to room temperature before storing it in an airtight container.

Nutritional Information (Per Serving): Calories: 322 / Fat: 17g / Protein: 11g / Carbohydrates: 35g / Fiber: 6g

Air Fryer Breakfast Hash

Prep time: 10 minutes / Cook time: 30 minutes Serves 6

Ingredients:
• Oil spray
• 3 medium russet potatoes, diced (about 3 cups)
• 1/2 yellow onion, diced
• 1 green bell pepper, seeded and diced
• 30ml (2 tablespoons) olive oil
• 2 teaspoons granulated garlic
• 1 teaspoon salt
• 1/2 teaspoon freshly ground black pepper

Instructions:
1. Preheat the air fryer to 400ºF (204ºC). Line the air fryer basket with parchment paper and lightly spray with oil.
2. In a large bowl, toss together the diced potatoes, onion, bell pepper, and olive oil until well coated.
3. Sprinkle the granulated garlic, salt, and black pepper over the mixture and stir until evenly distributed.
4. Transfer the seasoned mixture to the prepared basket.
5. Air fry for 20 to 30 minutes, shaking or stirring every 10 minutes, until the hash is browned and crispy.
6. For extra crispiness, lightly spray the potatoes with oil each time you stir.
7. Once done, serve the breakfast hash hot and enjoy!

Nutritional Information (Per Serving): / Calories: 133 / Fat: 5g / Protein: 3g / Carbs: 21g / Fiber: 2g / Sodium: 395mg

Air Fryer Butternut Squash and Ricotta Frittata

Prep time: 10 minutes / Cook time: 33 minutes
Serves 2 to 3

Ingredients:
- 156g (1 cup) cubed (½-inch) butternut squash
- 30ml (2 tablespoons) olive oil
- Salt and pepper, to taste
- 4 fresh sage leaves, thinly sliced
- 6 large eggs, lightly beaten
- 120g (½ cup) ricotta cheese
- Cayenne pepper

Instructions:
1. In a bowl, toss the butternut squash cubes with olive oil, salt, and pepper until evenly coated. Sprinkle the thinly sliced sage leaves on the bottom of a cake pan, then arrange the squash on top. Place the pan in the air fryer and bake at 400ºF (204ºC) for 10 minutes. Stir to incorporate the sage, then continue cooking until the squash is tender and lightly caramelized, about 3 minutes more.
2. Pour the beaten eggs over the cooked squash, dot with spoonfuls of ricotta cheese, and sprinkle with cayenne pepper. Bake at 300ºF (149ºC) until the eggs are set and the frittata is golden brown on top, approximately 20 minutes. Remove the pan from the air fryer and slice the frittata into wedges before serving.

Nutritional Information (Per Serving): Calories: 289 / Fat: 22g / Protein: 18g / Carbs: 5g / Fiber: 1g / Sodium: 184mg

Air Fryer Mini Shrimp Frittata

Prep time: 15 minutes / Cook time: 20 minutes
Serves 4

Ingredients:
- Olive oil, for spraying
- ½ small red bell pepper, finely diced
- 1 teaspoon minced garlic
- 113g (4-ounce) can of tiny shrimp, drained
- Salt and freshly ground black pepper, to taste
- 4 eggs, beaten
- 4 teaspoons ricotta cheese

Instructions:
1. Lightly spray four ramekins with olive oil.
2. Heat 1 teaspoon of olive oil in a medium skillet over medium-low heat. Sauté the diced bell pepper and minced garlic until the pepper is soft, approximately 5 minutes.
3. Add the drained shrimp to the skillet, season with salt and pepper, and cook until warmed through, about 1 to 2 minutes. Remove from heat.
4. Stir the beaten eggs into the shrimp mixture until well combined.
5. Divide the mixture evenly among the four ramekins.
6. Place two ramekins in the air fryer basket and cook at 350ºF (177ºC) for 6 minutes.
7. Remove the air fryer basket, stir the mixture in each ramekin, and top each frittata with 1 teaspoon of ricotta cheese.
8. Return the air fryer basket to the air fryer and cook until the eggs are set and the top is lightly browned, approximately 4 to 5 minutes.
9. Repeat the process with the remaining two ramekins.

Nutritional Information (Per Serving): Calories: 114 / Fat: 6g / Protein: 12g / Carbs: 1g / Fiber: 0g / Sodium: 314mg

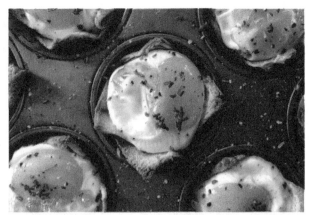

Air Fryer Spinach and Mushroom Mini Quiche

Prep time: 10 minutes / Cook time: 15 minutes
Serves 4

Ingredients:
• Olive oil, for spraying
• 1 cup (150g) coarsely chopped mushrooms
• 1 cup (30g) fresh baby spinach, shredded
• 4 eggs, beaten
• 1/2 cup (60g) shredded Cheddar cheese
• 1/2 cup (60g) shredded Mozzarella cheese
• 1/4 teaspoon salt
• 1/4 teaspoon black pepper

Instructions:
1. Lightly spray 4 silicone baking cups with olive oil.
2. Heat 1 teaspoon of olive oil in a medium sauté pan over medium heat. Sauté the chopped mushrooms until soft, about 3 to 4 minutes.
3. Add the shredded baby spinach to the pan and cook until wilted, about 1 to 2 minutes. Set aside.
4. In a medium bowl, whisk together the beaten eggs, Cheddar cheese, Mozzarella cheese, salt, and black pepper.
5. Gently fold the sautéed mushrooms and spinach into the egg mixture until well combined.
6. Divide the mixture evenly among the silicone baking cups.
7. Place the baking cups into the air fryer basket and cook at 350ºF (177ºC) for 5 minutes. Stir the mixture in each cup slightly and continue to cook until the egg has set, an additional 3 to 5 minutes.

Nutritional Information (Per Serving): Calories: 156 / Fat: 10g / Protein: 14g / Carbs: 2g / Fiber: 1g / Sodium: 411mg

Air Fryer Italian Egg Cups

Prep time: 5 minutes / Cook time: 10 minutes
Serves 4

Ingredients:
• Olive oil
• 1 cup (240ml) marinara sauce
• 4 eggs
• 4 tablespoons shredded Mozzarella cheese
• 4 teaspoons grated Parmesan cheese
• Salt and freshly ground black pepper, to taste
• Chopped fresh basil, for garnish

Instructions:
1. Lightly coat 4 individual ramekins with olive oil.
2. Pour 1/4 cup of marinara sauce into each ramekin.
3. Carefully crack one egg into each ramekin over the marinara sauce.
4. Sprinkle 1 tablespoon of Mozzarella cheese and 1 tablespoon of Parmesan cheese on top of each egg. Season with salt and pepper.
5. Cover each ramekin with aluminum foil and place two ramekins in the air fryer basket.
6. Air fry at 350ºF (177ºC) for 5 minutes, then remove the aluminum foil. Continue to air fry until the top is lightly browned and the egg white is cooked, for an additional 2 to 4 minutes. If you prefer a firmer yolk, cook for 3 to 5 more minutes.
7. Repeat the process with the remaining two ramekins. Garnish with chopped fresh basil before serving.

Nutritional Information (Per Serving): Calories: 123 / Fat: 7g / Protein: 9g / Carbs: 6g / Fiber: 1g / Sodium: 84mg

Air Fryer Mexican Breakfast Pepper Rings

Prep time: 5 minutes / Cook time: 10 minutes
Serves 4

Ingredients:
- Olive oil
- 1 large red, yellow, or orange bell pepper, sliced into four 3/4-inch rings
- 4 eggs
- Salt and freshly ground black pepper, to taste
- 2 teaspoons salsa

Instructions:
1. Preheat your air fryer to 350°F (177°C). Lightly coat a baking pan with olive oil.
2. Arrange 2 bell pepper rings on the prepared pan. Crack one egg into each pepper ring. Season with salt and black pepper.
3. Spoon 1/2 teaspoon of salsa on top of each egg.
4. Place the pan in the air fryer basket. Air fry until the egg yolk reaches your desired consistency, approximately 5 to 6 minutes for slightly runny yolks or 8 to 10 minutes for fully cooked yolks.
5. Repeat the process with the remaining 2 pepper rings. Serve hot.

Nutritional Information (Per Serving): Calories: 76 / Fat: 4g / Protein: 6g / Carbs: 3g / Fiber: 1g / Sodium: 83mg

Air Fryer Veggie Frittata

Prep time: 7 minutes / Cook time: 21 to 23 minutes
Serves 2

Ingredients:
- Avocado oil spray
- 1/4 cup (40g) diced red onion
- 1/4 cup (40g) diced red bell pepper
- 1/4 cup (40g) finely chopped broccoli
- 4 large eggs
- 3 ounces (85 g) shredded sharp Cheddar cheese, divided
- 1/2 teaspoon dried thyme
- Sea salt and freshly ground black pepper, to taste

Instructions:
1. Begin by spraying a pan with avocado oil. Place the diced red onion, red bell pepper, and chopped broccoli in the pan. Put the pan in the air fryer and set it to 350°F (177°C). Allow the vegetables to cook for 5 minutes.
2. While the vegetables are cooking, beat the eggs in a medium-sized bowl. Stir in half of the shredded Cheddar cheese, and season the mixture with dried thyme, sea salt, and freshly ground black pepper.
3. Once the vegetables are done cooking, add the beaten egg mixture to the pan. Sprinkle the remaining shredded Cheddar cheese on top. Set the air fryer to 350°F (177°C) again and bake the frittata for 16 to 18 minutes, or until it is cooked through.

Nutritional Information (Per Serving): Calories: 326 / Fat: 23g / Protein: 24g / Carbs: 4g / Fiber: 1g / Sodium: 156mg

Air Fryer Smoky Sausage Patties

Prep time: 30 minutes / Cook time: 9 minutes
Serves 8

Ingredients:
- 1 pound (454 g) ground pork
- 1 tablespoon coconut aminos
- 2 teaspoons liquid smoke
- 1 teaspoon dried sage
- 1 teaspoon sea salt
- 1/2 teaspoon fennel seeds
- 1/2 teaspoon dried thyme
- 1/2 teaspoon freshly ground black pepper
- 1/4 teaspoon cayenne pepper

Instructions:
1. In a large bowl, combine the ground pork, coconut aminos, liquid smoke, sage, sea salt, fennel seeds, thyme, black pepper, and cayenne pepper. Mix well until the seasonings are evenly distributed throughout the meat.
2. Shape the mixture into 8 equal-size patties, making a dent in the center of each with your thumb. Place the patties on a plate, cover with plastic wrap, and refrigerate for at least 30 minutes.
3. Preheat the air fryer to 400°F (204°C). Place the patties in a single layer in the air fryer basket, working in batches if necessary to avoid overcrowding.
4. Air fry the patties for 5 minutes, then flip them and cook for an additional 4 minutes or until fully cooked through.
5. Serve hot and enjoy!

*Nutritional Information (Per Serving):*Calories: 70 / Fat: 2g / Protein: 12g / Carbs: 0g / Fiber: 0g / Sodium: 329mg

Air Fryer Spinach and Feta Egg Bake

Prep time: 7 minutes / Cook time: 23 to 25 minutes
Serves 2

Ingredients:
- Avocado oil spray
- 1/3 cup (40g) diced red onion
- 1 cup (150g) frozen chopped spinach, thawed and drained
- 4 large eggs
- 1/4 cup (60ml) heavy (whipping) cream
- Sea salt and freshly ground black pepper, to taste
- 1/4 teaspoon cayenne pepper
- 1/2 cup (75g) crumbled feta cheese
- 1/4 cup (25g) shredded Parmesan cheese

Instructions:
1. Spray a deep pan with avocado oil. Spread diced red onion in the pan and place it in the air fryer basket. Set the air fryer to 350°F (177°C) and bake for 7 minutes.
2. Sprinkle thawed and drained chopped spinach over the cooked onion.
3. In a medium bowl, beat the eggs, heavy cream, sea salt, black pepper, and cayenne pepper. Pour this mixture over the vegetables in the pan.
4. Top the mixture with crumbled feta cheese and shredded Parmesan cheese. Bake for 16 to 18 minutes until the eggs are set and lightly browned.

*Nutritional Information (Per Serving):*Calories: 366 / Fat: 26g / Protein: 25g / Carbs: 8g / Fiber: 3g / Sodium: 520mg

Air Fryer Jalapeño Popper Egg Cups

Prep time: 10 minutes / Cook time: 10 minutes
Serves 2

Ingredients:
- 4 large eggs
- 1/4 cup (60g) chopped pickled jalapeños
- 2 ounces (57g) full-fat cream cheese
- 1/2 cup (56g) shredded sharp Cheddar cheese

Instructions:
1. Beat the eggs in a medium bowl, then pour the mixture into four silicone muffin cups.
2. In a large microwave-safe bowl, combine the chopped pickled jalapeños, cream cheese, and shredded sharp Cheddar cheese. Microwave for 30 seconds and stir until well combined. Spoon approximately 1/4 of the mixture into the center of each egg cup.
3. Place the egg cups into the air fryer basket.
4. Adjust the air fryer temperature to 320ºF (160ºC) and bake for 10 minutes.
5. Serve the jalapeño popper egg cups warm.

Nutritional Information (Per Serving):Calories: 375 / Fat: 30g / Protein: 23g / Carbs: 3g / Fiber: 0g / Sodium: 445mg

Air Fryer Buffalo Egg Cups

Prep time: 10 minutes / Cook time: 15 minutes
Serves 2

Ingredients:
- 4 large eggs
- 2 ounces (57g) full-fat cream cheese
- 2 tablespoons buffalo sauce
- 1/2 cup (56g) shredded sharp Cheddar cheese

Instructions:
1. Crack the eggs into two ramekins.
2. In a small microwave-safe bowl, combine the full-fat cream cheese, buffalo sauce, and shredded sharp Cheddar cheese. Microwave for 20 seconds, then stir until well mixed. Spoon the mixture into each ramekin on top of the eggs.
3. Place the ramekins into the air fryer basket.
4. Adjust the air fryer temperature to 320ºF (160ºC) and bake for 15 minutes.
5. Serve the buffalo egg cups warm.

Nutritional Information (Per Serving):Calories: 354 / Fat: 29g / Protein: 21g / Carbs: 3g / Fiber: 0g / Sodium: 343mg

Savoury Oats Greek Style

Prep time: 5 minutes / Cook time: 19 minutes
Serves 4

Ingredients:
- 1 cup (200g) porridge oats
- 1/2 cup (100g) Kalamata olives, stoned and sliced
- 3/4 cup (200ml) vegetable broth
- 1/3 cup (100ml) tomato sauce
- A large handful of baby spinach
- 3/4 cup (200ml) Greek-style yoghurt
- 1 tsp olive oil
- Flaky sea salt and ground black pepper, to taste

Instructions:
1. Preheat your air fryer to 180 degrees C.
2. Brush the inside of a baking tin with olive oil.
3. In a mixing bowl, thoroughly combine the porridge oats, vegetable broth, tomato sauce, Kalamata olives, salt, and pepper.
4. Spoon the mixture into the prepared baking tin.
5. Bake the porridge for 10 minutes.
6. After 10 minutes, add the baby spinach to the baking tin, gently stir to combine, and continue cooking for a further 9 minutes.
7. Divide the cooked porridge between four serving bowls.
8. Garnish each serving with a dollop of Greek-style yoghurt.
9. Enjoy your nutritious meal!

Nutritional Information (Per Serving): Calories: 225 / Fat: 9.1g / Carbs: 39.3g / Fiber: 9g / Protein: 16.1g

Mediterranean Scrambled Eggs

Prep time: 10 minutes / Cook time: 14 minutes
Serves 4

Ingredients:
- 6 large eggs
- 1 tbsp olive oil
- 3.5 oz (100g) feta cheese
- 2 tbsp Kalamata olives, stoned and halved
- A large handful of baby spinach
- 1 spring onion, thinly sliced (green and white parts separated)
- 1 tbsp fresh parsley leaves, chopped
- 1/2 tsp red pepper flakes, crushed
- Sea salt and ground black pepper, to taste

Instructions:
1. Preheat your Air Fryer to 190 degrees C.
2. In a mixing bowl, whisk the eggs until pale and frothy.
3. Fold in the baby spinach, white parts of the spring onion, parsley leaves, red pepper flakes, sea salt, and black pepper. Gently stir to combine.
4. Lightly grease a baking tray and spoon the egg mixture into it.
5. Cook the scrambled eggs in the preheated Air Fryer for about 14 minutes, or until they reach your desired level of doneness.
6. Once cooked, sprinkle the scrambled eggs with the green parts of the spring onion, crumbled feta cheese, and halved Kalamata olives.
7. Serve and enjoy your Mediterranean-inspired scrambled eggs!

Nutritional Information (Per Serving): Calories: 225 / Fat: 16.4g / Carbs: 4.6g / Fiber: 4.4g / Protein: 1.3g

Tuna and Sweetcorn Fritters

Prep time: 10 minutes / Cook time: 20 minutes
Serves 4

Ingredients:

- 1 egg
- 7/8 cup (200g) canned tuna, drained
- 1/2 cup (100g) sweet corn kernels, thawed
- 6 tbsp Italian breadcrumbs
- 2 tbsp pecorino cheese, grated
- 1 small red onion, chopped
- 2 tbsp olive oil
- 1/2 tsp dried oregano
- 1 tsp dried basil
- 1 heaped tsp dried rosemary
- Sea salt and ground black pepper, to taste

Instructions:

1. Whisk the egg until pale and frothy in a mixing bowl.
2. Fold in the canned tuna, sweet corn kernels, Italian breadcrumbs, grated pecorino cheese, chopped red onion, dried oregano, dried basil, dried rosemary, sea salt, and ground black pepper. Stir well to combine.
3. Shape the mixture into patties, flattening them down with the back of a spoon into disc shapes.
4. Lower the fritters into a parchment-lined cooking basket.
5. Cook the fritters in the air fryer at 190 degrees C for about 10 minutes.
6. After 10 minutes, carefully turn the fritters over and cook for a further 10 minutes, until thoroughly cooked.
7. Serve hot and enjoy your delicious tuna and sweet corn fritters!

Nutritional Information (Per Serving): Calories: 229 / Fat: 11.6g / Carbs: 14.4g / Fiber: 2g / Protein: 16.4g

Classic Savoury Muffins

Preparation time: 15 minutes / Cooking time: 20 minutes

Ingredients:

- 1 large egg
- 1 cup (250 ml) whole milk
- 1/4 cup (50g) Greek yoghurt
- 1/4 cup (60ml) olive oil
- 2 1/4 cups (300g) plain flour
- 1 tsp baking powder
- 1/2 tsp baking soda
- 1/2 tsp salt
- 1 green onion, sliced
- 1 garlic clove, smashed
- 3.5 oz (100g) Kalamata olives, stoned and sliced

Instructions:

1. Preheat your Air Fryer to 175 degrees C.
2. Brush a muffin tin with cooking oil, and place 6 muffin cases inside.
3. In a large mixing bowl, beat the egg until pale and frothy. Gradually add the whole milk, Greek yoghurt, and olive oil, stirring continuously.
4. Gradually stir in the plain flour, baking powder, baking soda, and salt, in the order listed above, until well combined.
5. Use a wire whisk to stir until a smooth batter forms, being careful not to overmix.
6. Fold in the sliced green onion, smashed garlic, and sliced Kalamata olives, gently stirring to combine.
7. Spoon the batter into the prepared muffin tin, dividing it evenly among the 6 muffin cases.
8. Place the muffin tin in the preheated Air Fryer and cook the muffins for approximately 20 minutes, or until they are golden brown and cooked through.
9. Allow the muffins to cool in the tin for about 10 minutes before carefully unmolding and serving.
10. Enjoy your delicious classic savoury muffins!

Nutritional Information (Per Serving): Calories: 349 / Fat: 15.1g / Carbs: 44.4g / Fiber: 2g / Protein: 8.4g

Authentic Italian Frittata

Prep time: 5 minutes / Cook time: 15 minutes
Serves 4

Ingredients:
- 6 medium eggs, beaten
- 6 heaped tbsp (about 90g) whole-milk ricotta cheese, crumbled
- 1 small onion, chopped
- 3.5 oz (100g) chestnut mushrooms, sliced
- 3.5 oz (100g) bag spinach
- 1 medium tomato, diced
- 1 tbsp olive oil

Instructions:
1. Preheat your Air Fryer to 180 degrees C.
2. In a mixing bowl, whisk the eggs until frothy.
3. Fold in the chopped onion, sliced chestnut mushrooms, bag of spinach, diced tomato, crumbled whole-milk ricotta cheese, and olive oil. Whisk until all ingredients are well incorporated.
4. Lightly oil a baking tray and spoon the frittata mixture into it, spreading it evenly.
5. Place the baking tray in the preheated Air Fryer and bake the frittata for 15 minutes, or until it is set and golden brown on top.
6. Once cooked, carefully remove the frittata from the Air Fryer and allow it to cool slightly before slicing and serving.
7. Enjoy your authentic Italian frittata!

Nutritional Information (Per Serving): Calories: 189 / Fat: 12.5g / Carbs: 5.9g / Fiber: 1.5g / Protein: 12.2g

Greek Breakfast Casserole

Prep time: 10 minutes / Cook time: 30 minutes
Serves 4

Ingredients:
- 1 tbsp olive oil
- 7 oz (200g) loukaniko (Greek sausage), sliced
- 1 small red onion, sliced
- 6 large eggs, beaten
- 3.5 oz (100g) halloumi cheese, crumbled

Instructions:
1. Preheat your Air Fryer to 180 degrees C.
2. Brush the bottom and sides of a baking tray with olive oil.
3. Arrange the sliced loukaniko (Greek sausage) in the bottom of the prepared baking tray.
4. Top the sausage with the sliced red onion.
5. Pour the beaten eggs evenly over the sausage and onion.
6. Bake the breakfast casserole in the preheated Air Fryer for 15 minutes.
7. After 15 minutes, sprinkle the crumbled halloumi cheese over the casserole.
8. Continue to bake for a further 15 minutes, until the cheese is melted and bubbly.
9. Once cooked, remove the casserole from the Air Fryer and let it cool slightly before serving.
10. Enjoy your delicious Greek breakfast casserole!

Nutritional Information (Per Serving): Calories: 356 / Fat: 27g / Carbs: 4.7g / Fiber: 0.3g / Protein: 21.2g

Chapter 2: Poultry Recipes

Honey-Glazed Chicken Thighs

Prep time: 5 minutes / Cook time: 14 minutes
Serves 4

Ingredients:
- Oil, for spraying
- 4 boneless, skinless chicken thighs, fat trimmed
- 3 tablespoons (45ml) soy sauce
- 1 tablespoon (15ml) balsamic vinegar
- 2 teaspoons (10g) honey
- 2 teaspoons (6g) minced garlic
- 1 teaspoon (2g) ground ginger

Instructions:
1. Preheat the air fryer to 400°F (204°C). Line the air fryer basket with parchment paper and lightly spray with oil.
2. Place the chicken thighs in the prepared basket.
3. Cook for 7 minutes, then flip the chicken thighs and cook for another 7 minutes or until the internal temperature reaches 165°F (74°C) and the juices run clear.
4. In a small saucepan, combine the soy sauce, balsamic vinegar, honey, minced garlic, and ground ginger. Cook over low heat for 1 to 2 minutes until warmed through.
5. Transfer the cooked chicken thighs to a serving plate and drizzle with the sauce just before serving.

*Nutritional Information (Per Serving):*Calories: 286 / Fat: 10g / Protein: 39g / Carbs: 7g / Fiber: 0g / Sodium: 365mg

Turkey Tenderloin

Prep time: 20 minutes / Cook time: 30 minutes
Serves 4

Ingredients:
- Olive oil
- 1½ pounds (680g) turkey breast tenderloin
- ½ teaspoon (2.5g) paprika
- ½ teaspoon (2.5g) garlic powder
- ½ teaspoon (2.5g) salt
- ½ teaspoon (2.5g) freshly ground black pepper
- Pinch of cayenne pepper

Instructions:
1. Lightly spray the air fryer basket with olive oil.
2. In a small bowl, mix together the paprika, garlic powder, salt, black pepper, and cayenne pepper.
3. Rub the spice mixture evenly over the turkey tenderloin.
4. Place the seasoned turkey tenderloin in the air fryer basket and lightly spray the top with olive oil.
5. Air fry at 370°F (188°C) for 15 minutes. Flip the turkey over, lightly spray with olive oil, and continue air frying until the internal temperature reaches at least 170°F (77°C), about 10 to 15 minutes more.
6. Allow the turkey to rest for 10 minutes before slicing and serving.

*Nutritional Information (Per Serving):*Calories: 196 / Fat: 3g / Protein: 40g / Carbs: 1g / Fiber: 0g / Sodium: 483mg

Buffalo Chicken Cheese Sticks

Prep time: 5 minutes / Cook time: 8 minutes
Serves 2

Ingredients:
- 100g shredded cooked chicken (about 1/2 cup)
- 100g shredded Mozzarella cheese (about 1 cup)
- 60ml buffalo sauce (1/4 cup)
- 1 large egg
- 25g crumbled feta cheese (about 1/4 cup)

Instructions:
1. In a large bowl, combine shredded chicken, shredded Mozzarella cheese, buffalo sauce, and beaten egg. Mix until well combined.
2. Cut a piece of parchment paper to fit the air fryer basket and press the chicken and cheese mixture into a ½-inch-thick circle on the parchment paper.
3. Sprinkle the crumbled feta cheese evenly over the top of the mixture.
4. Place the parchment paper with the chicken and cheese mixture into the air fryer basket.
5. Adjust the air fryer temperature to 400ºF (204ºC) and cook for 8 minutes.
6. After 5 minutes of cooking, carefully flip over the cheese mixture using a spatula.
7. Once cooked, remove from the air fryer and let it cool for 5 minutes before cutting into sticks. Serve warm.

Nutritional Information (Per Serving):Calories: 413 / Fat: 25g / Protein: 43g / Carbs: 3g / Fiber: 0g / Sodium: 453mg

Cauliflower Pizza

Prep time: 10 minutes / Cook time: 25 minutes
Serves 2

Ingredients:
- 1 (12-ounce / 340-g) bag frozen riced cauliflower
- 80g shredded Mozzarella cheese (about 1/3 cup)
- 30g almond flour (about 1/4 cup)
- 30g grated Parmesan cheese (about 1/4 cup)
- 1 large egg   • ½ teaspoon salt
- 1 teaspoon garlic powder • 1 teaspoon dried oregano
- 4 tablespoons no-sugar-added marinara sauce, divided
- 113g fresh Mozzarella, chopped, divided
- 110g cooked chicken breast, chopped, divided
- 75g chopped cherry tomatoes, divided (about 1/2 cup)
- 15g fresh baby arugula, divided (about 1/4 cup)

Instructions:
1. Preheat the air fryer to 400ºF (204ºC) and cut 4 sheets of parchment paper to fit the basket. Lightly brush them with olive oil.
2. Microwave the cauliflower in a large glass bowl according to package instructions. Transfer it to a clean towel, squeeze out excess moisture, and return it to the bowl. Add shredded Mozzarella, almond flour, Parmesan, egg, salt, garlic powder, and oregano. Mix well.
3. Divide the dough into two portions and shape each into a 7 to 8-inch disk. Air fry for 15 minutes until the crust begins to brown. Let cool for 5 minutes.
4. Transfer the crust to a baking sheet lined with parchment paper. Cover with another sheet of parchment paper, flip it, and return it to the air fryer basket. Remove the top parchment paper and air fry for another 15 minutes until the top is browned.
5. Spread 2 tablespoons of marinara sauce on each crust, followed by half of the fresh Mozzarella, chicken, cherry tomatoes, and arugula. Air fry for 5 to 10 minutes until the cheese melts and begins to brown. Let it cool for 10 minutes before serving. Repeat for the second pizza.

Nutritional Information (Per Serving):Calories: 655 / Fat: 35g / Protein: 67g / Carbs: 20g / Fiber: 7g / Sodium: 741mg

Chicken Lettuce Wraps

Prep time: 15 minutes / Cook time: 14 minutes
Serves 4

Ingredients:
- 454g chicken breast tenders, chopped into bite-size pieces (1 pound)
- ½ onion, thinly sliced
- 1 red bell pepper, seeded and thinly sliced (about ½ cup)
- 1 green bell pepper, seeded and thinly sliced (about ½ cup)
- 15ml olive oil (1 tablespoon)
- 1 tablespoon fajita seasoning
- 5g kosher salt (1 teaspoon)
- Juice of ½ lime
- 8 large lettuce leaves
- 240g prepared guacamole (1 cup)

Instructions:
1. Preheat the air fryer to 400ºF (204ºC).
2. In a large bowl, mix the chicken, onion, and peppers. Drizzle with olive oil and toss to coat. Add fajita seasoning and salt, toss again.
3. Arrange chicken and vegetables in a single layer in the air fryer basket. Cook for 14 minutes or until vegetables are tender and chicken reaches 165ºF (74ºC), shaking the basket halfway.
4. Transfer to a serving platter, drizzle with lime juice. Serve with lettuce leaves and top with guacamole.

Nutritional Information (Per Serving): Calories: 273 / Fat: 15g / Protein: 27g / Carbs: 9g / Fiber: 5g / Sodium: 723mg

Chicken Patties

Prep time: 15 minutes / Cook time: 12 minutes
Serves 4

Ingredients:
- 454g ground chicken thigh meat (1 pound)
- 120g shredded Mozzarella cheese (1/2 cup)
- 1 teaspoon dried parsley
- ½ teaspoon garlic powder
- ¼ teaspoon onion powder
- 1 large egg
- 57g finely ground pork rinds (2 ounces)

Instructions:
1. In a large bowl, combine ground chicken, Mozzarella cheese, parsley, garlic powder, and onion powder. Form the mixture into four patties.
2. Place the patties in the freezer for 15 to 20 minutes until they firm up slightly.
3. Whisk the egg in a medium bowl. Place the ground pork rinds in a separate large bowl.
4. Dip each chicken patty into the egg, then coat with ground pork rinds.
5. Place the coated patties in the air fryer basket.
6. Set the air fryer to 360ºF (182ºC) and cook for 12 minutes.
7. Check that the patties are firm and reach an internal temperature of 165ºF (74ºC). Serve immediately.

Nutritional Information (Per Serving): Calories: 265 / Fat: 15g / Protein: 29g / Carbs: 1g / Fiber: 0g / Sodium: 285mg

Air Fryer Pork Rind Fried Chicken

Prep time: 30 minutes / Cook time: 20 minutes
Serves 4

Ingredients:
- 1/4 cup (60ml) buffalo sauce
- 4 boneless, skinless chicken breasts (about 454g or 113g each)
- 1/2 teaspoon (2.5ml) paprika
- 1/2 teaspoon (2.5ml) garlic powder
- 1/4 teaspoon (1.25ml) ground black pepper
- 2 ounces (57g) plain pork rinds, finely crushed

Instructions:
1. In a large sealable bowl or bag, pour in the buffalo sauce. Add the chicken breasts and toss to coat. Seal the bowl or bag and place it in the refrigerator to marinate for at least 30 minutes, up to overnight.
2. Remove the chicken from the marinade without shaking off the excess sauce. Sprinkle both sides of the chicken breasts with paprika, garlic powder, and black pepper.
3. Place the finely crushed pork rinds in a large bowl. Press each chicken breast into the pork rinds, coating evenly on both sides.
4. Arrange the coated chicken breasts in the air fryer basket. Set the temperature to 400°F (204°C) and cook for 20 minutes, flipping the chicken halfway through the cooking time. Ensure that the chicken reaches an internal temperature of at least 165°F (74°C).
5. Once done, the chicken will be golden brown. Serve warm.

Nutritional Information (Per Serving): Calories: 217 / Fat: 8g / Protein: 35g / Carbs: 1g / Fiber: 0g / Sodium: 400mg

Air Fryer Cilantro Lime Chicken Thighs

Prep time: 15 minutes / Cook time: 22 minutes
Serves 4

Ingredients:
- 4 bone-in, skin-on chicken thighs
- 1 teaspoon (5g) baking powder
- 1/2 teaspoon (1.5g) garlic powder
- 2 teaspoons (4g) chili powder
- 1 teaspoon (2.5g) cumin
- 2 medium limes
- 1/4 cup (15g) chopped fresh cilantro

Instructions:
1. Start by patting the chicken thighs dry and then sprinkle them with baking powder.
2. In a small bowl, combine the garlic powder, chili powder, and cumin. Sprinkle this mixture evenly over the chicken thighs, ensuring it gets under the skin as well.
3. Cut one lime in half and squeeze the juice over the chicken thighs.
4. Place the seasoned chicken thighs into the air fryer basket.
5. Set the air fryer temperature to 380°F (193°C) and cook the chicken thighs for 22 minutes.
6. Once cooked, cut the remaining lime into four wedges for serving. Garnish the cooked chicken thighs with the lime wedges and freshly chopped cilantro.

Nutritional Information (Per Serving): Calories: 445 / Fat: 32g / Protein: 32g / Carbs: 6g / Fiber: 2g / Sodium: 198mg

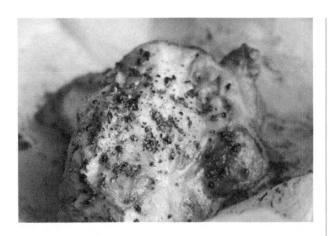

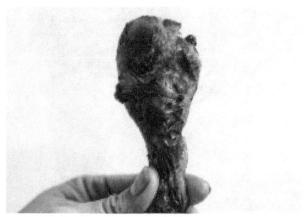

Air Fryer Chicken Thighs with Cilantro

Prep time: 15 minutes / Cook time: 25 minutes
Serves 4

Ingredients:
- 8 bone-in chicken thighs, skin on
- 1 tablespoon (15ml) olive oil
- Juice of 1/2 lime
- 1 tablespoon (15ml) coconut aminos
- 1 1/2 teaspoons Montreal chicken seasoning
- 2 tablespoons (8g) chopped fresh cilantro

Instructions:
1. In a gallon-size resealable bag, combine the olive oil, lime juice, coconut aminos, and Montreal chicken seasoning. Add the chicken thighs to the bag, seal it, and massage to ensure the chicken is evenly coated. Refrigerate for at least 2 hours, preferably overnight.
2. Preheat your air fryer to 400°F (204°C).
3. Remove the chicken thighs from the marinade and arrange them in a single layer in the air fryer basket. Cook for 20 to 25 minutes, flipping halfway through, until the internal temperature reaches 165°F (74°C).
4. Transfer the cooked chicken thighs to a serving platter and sprinkle with chopped cilantro before serving.

Nutritional Information (Per Serving): Calories: 692 / Fat: 53g / Protein: 49g / Carbs: 2g / Fiber: 0g / Sodium: 242mg

Air Fryer Teriyaki Chicken Legs

Prep time: 12 minutes / Cook time: 18 to 20 minutes
Serves 2

Ingredients:
- 4 chicken legs
- 4 tablespoons (60ml) teriyaki sauce
- 1 tablespoon (15ml) orange juice
- 1 teaspoon smoked paprika
- Cooking spray

Instructions:
1. In a small bowl, combine the teriyaki sauce, orange juice, and smoked paprika. Brush this mixture evenly on all sides of the chicken legs.
2. Lightly spray the air fryer basket with cooking spray and place the chicken legs inside.
3. Air fry at 360°F (182°C) for 6 minutes. Then, turn the chicken legs, baste them with the sauce, and cook for an additional 6 minutes. Repeat the process, turning and basting every 6 minutes, until the chicken is cooked through and the juices run clear when pierced with a fork.

Nutritional Information (Per Serving): Calories: 392 / Fat: 13g / Protein: 59g / Carbs: 7g / Fiber: 1g / Sodium: 641mg

Air Fryer Pecan Turkey Cutlets

Prep time: 10 minutes / Cook time: 10 to 12 minutes
Serves 4

Ingredients:
- ¾ cup (75g) panko bread crumbs
- ½ cup (60g) pecans • ¼ cup (30g) cornstarch
- 1 egg, beaten • ¼ teaspoon salt
- ¼ teaspoon pepper • ¼ teaspoon dry mustard
- ¼ teaspoon poultry seasoning
- 1 pound (454g) turkey cutlets, ½-inch thick
- Salt and pepper, to taste
- Oil for misting or cooking spray

Instructions:
1. In a food processor, combine the panko crumbs, ¼ teaspoon salt, ¼ teaspoon pepper, dry mustard, and poultry seasoning. Pulse until the crumbs are finely crushed. Add the pecans and pulse briefly until the nuts are finely chopped.
2. Preheat your air fryer to 360ºF (182ºC).
3. Place the cornstarch in one shallow dish and the beaten egg in another. Transfer the coating mixture from the food processor into a third shallow dish.
4. Season the turkey cutlets with salt and pepper to taste.
5. Dredge each cutlet in the cornstarch, shaking off any excess. Then dip it in the beaten egg and coat it well with the crumb mixture, pressing gently to adhere. Spray both sides of the coated cutlets with oil or cooking spray.
6. Arrange 2 cutlets in the air fryer basket in a single layer. Cook for 10 to 12 minutes, or until the juices run clear.
7. Repeat the cooking process with the remaining cutlets.

Nutritional Information (Per Serving): Calories: 340 / Fat: 13g / Protein: 31g / Carbs: 24g / Fiber: 4g / Sodium: 447mg

Taco Chicken

Prep time: 10 minutes / Cook time: 23 minutes
Serves 4

Ingredients:
- 2 large eggs • 1 tablespoon water
- Fine sea salt and ground black pepper, to taste
- 1 cup (115g) pork dust • 1 teaspoon ground cumin
- 1 teaspoon smoked paprika
- 4 boneless, skinless chicken breasts or thighs (about 5 ounces / 142g each), pounded to ¼ inch thick
- 1 cup (240g) salsa • Avocado oil spray
- 1 cup (113g) shredded Monterey Jack cheese (omit for dairy-free)
- Sprig of fresh cilantro, for garnish (optional)

Instructions:
1. Spray the air fryer basket with avocado oil and preheat the air fryer to 400ºF (204ºC).
2. In a shallow baking dish, whisk together the eggs, water, salt, and pepper. In another shallow dish, combine the pork dust, cumin, and smoked paprika.
3. Season the chicken breasts or thighs with salt and pepper. Dip each piece of chicken in the egg mixture, letting any excess drip off, then coat both sides with the pork dust mixture.
4. Place the breaded chicken in the air fryer basket and spray with avocado oil. Repeat with the remaining chicken.
5. Air fry the chicken for 20 minutes, flipping halfway through, until the internal temperature reaches 165ºF (74ºC) and the breading is golden brown.
6. Top each chicken piece with ¼ cup of salsa and ¼ cup of shredded cheese. Return to the air fryer and cook for an additional 3 minutes, or until the cheese is melted.
7. Garnish with cilantro before serving, if desired.
8. Store any leftovers in an airtight container in the refrigerator for up to 4 days. Reheat in a preheated 400ºF (204ºC) air fryer for 5 minutes, or until warmed through.

Nutritional Information (Per Serving): / Calories: 360 / Fat: 15g / Protein: 20g / Carbs: 4g / Fiber: 1g / Sodium: 490mg

Chicken Mini Meatloaves

Prep time: 10 minutes / Cook time: 20 minutes
Serves 4

Ingredients:
• 21.2 oz (600g) chicken mince
• 2.1 oz (60g) breadcrumbs
• 1 medium egg, beaten
• 2 spring onions, sliced
• 2 cloves garlic, minced
• Sea salt and ground black pepper, to taste
• 2 tbsp tomato purée
• 1 tsp ground cumin
• 1 tsp Dijon mustard
• 1 tbsp honey

Instructions:
1. In a mixing bowl, thoroughly combine the chicken mince, breadcrumbs, beaten egg, sliced spring onions, minced garlic, sea salt, and ground black pepper.
2. Scrape the mixture into lightly oiled muffin cases.
3. Lower the muffin cases into the cooking basket of the Air Fryer.
4. Air fry the mini meatloaves at 180 degrees C for 10 minutes.
5. In a small mixing bowl, thoroughly combine the tomato purée, ground cumin, Dijon mustard, and honey.
6. Spread the tomato mixture on the top of each meatloaf.
7. Continue baking for a further 10 minutes, or until the centre of each meatloaf reaches 74 degrees C.
8. Serve the warm chicken mini meatloaves and enjoy!

Nutritional Information (Per Serving):Calories: 410 / Fat: 24.5g / Carbs: 15.5g / Fiber: 1.2g / Protein: 31.1g

Chicken Gyros with Tzatziki Sauce

Prep time: 10 minutes / Cook time: 25 minutes
Serves 4

Ingredients:
• 17.6 oz (500g) chicken breasts, boneless and skinless
• 1 tsp olive oil   • 2 tbsp yellow mustard
• 1 small bell pepper, deseeded and sliced
• 1 small red onion, thinly sliced
• Sea salt and ground black pepper, to taste
• 4 medium pita breads
Tzatziki Sauce:
• 1 small Greek cucumber, thinly sliced
• 3.4 fl oz (100ml) natural Greek yogurt
• 1 tbsp lemon juice   • 1 tbsp extra-virgin olive oil
• 1 garlic clove, smashed• 1 tbsp minced dill

Instructions:
1. Preheat the Air Fryer to 190 degrees C.
2. Pat the chicken breasts dry using tea towels. Toss the chicken breasts with olive oil, sea salt, and ground black pepper.
3. Cook the chicken in the Air Fryer for about 20 minutes, turning them over halfway through the cooking time, until they are cooked through.
4. Shred the cooked chicken breasts using two forks.
5. While the chicken is cooking, prepare the Tzatziki sauce by mixing all the ingredients together in a bowl.
6. Warm the pita bread in the Air Fryer at 160 degrees C for about 5 minutes.
7. To assemble the gyros, place a warm pita bread on a serving board, and add the shredded chicken, sliced bell pepper, sliced red onion, yellow mustard, and Tzatziki sauce.
8. Roll up the pita bread to enclose the filling.
9. Serve the chicken gyros immediately and enjoy!

Nutritional Information (Per Serving):Calories: 445 / Fat: 15.5g / Carbs: 39.1g / Fiber: 2.3g / Protein: 35.3g

Turkey and Beef Shish Kofta

Prep time: 10 minutes / Cook time: 20 minutes
Serves 4

Ingredients:
- 10.6 oz (300g) turkey mince (85% lean, 15% fat)
- 7 oz (200g) lean beef mince
- 1 thin slice of bread, soaked in water until tender
- 1 tsp ground green cardamom
- 1/2 tsp ground sumac
- 1 bunch parsley, chopped
- 1 medium onion, chopped
- 2 garlic cloves, crushed
- Sea salt and ground black pepper, to taste
- 1 tsp olive oil

Instructions:
1. Soak 4 wooden skewers in water for about 30 minutes.
2. In a food processor, thoroughly combine the soaked bread, turkey mince, beef mince, green cardamom, sumac, chopped parsley, chopped onion, crushed garlic cloves, sea salt, and ground black pepper.
3. Take a fistful portion of the mixture and mold it onto a wooden skewer, forming it into a kofta shape.
4. Brush the bottom of the Air Fryer cooking basket with olive oil.
5. Place the koftas in the Air Fryer cooking basket.
6. Air fry the koftas at 180 degrees Celsius for about 20 minutes or until cooked through, turning them halfway through cooking.
7. Serve the shish kofta with toppings of your choice and enjoy!

Nutritional Information (Per Serving): Calories: 255 / Fat: 13.7g / Carbs: 7.9g / Fiber: 1.4g / Protein: 26.1g

Air Fryer Chicken Cacciatore

Prep time: 10 minutes / Cook time: 25 minutes
Serves 4

Ingredients:
- 1 tbsp olive oil, divided
- 21.2 oz (600g) skinless chicken thighs
- 10.6 oz (300g) mushrooms, sliced
- 1 medium onion, diced
- 2 fat garlic cloves, sliced
- 2 bell peppers, deseeded and sliced
- 1 tsp dried thyme   • 1 tsp dried oregano
- 3.4 fl oz (100ml) Mediterranean red wine
- 21.2 oz (600g) tomatoes, crushed
- Sea salt and ground black pepper, to taste

Instructions:
1. Preheat the Air Fryer to 195 degrees Celsius.
2. In a large bowl, toss the chicken thighs, mushrooms, diced onion, sliced garlic cloves, sliced bell peppers, dried thyme, dried oregano, Mediterranean red wine, crushed tomatoes, and half of the olive oil until well combined.
3. Grease a roasting tin lightly with the remaining olive oil.
4. Transfer the chicken mixture into the greased roasting tin.
5. Place the roasting tin into the Air Fryer cooking basket.
6. Air fry the chicken cacciatore at 195 degrees Celsius for 10 minutes.
7. Remove the roasting tin from the Air Fryer cooking basket and gently stir the mixture.
8. Return the roasting tin to the Air Fryer and continue to air fry for a further 15 minutes.
9. Serve the chicken cacciatore hot and enjoy!

Nutritional Information (Per Serving): Calories: 432 / Fat: 28.8g / Carbs: 15.1g / Fiber: 3.7g / Protein: 29.2g

Air Fryer Turkey Burgers

Prep time: 10 minutes / Cook time: 15 minutes
Serves 4

Ingredients:
- 21.2 oz (600g) turkey mince (85% lean, 15% fat)
- 1.4 oz (40g) instant oats
- 0.7 oz (20g) sun-dried tomatoes, chopped
- 1.4 oz (40g) feta cheese, crumbled
- 1 whole egg, beaten
- 1 medium onion, chopped
- 2 garlic cloves, crushed
- 1 tbsp fresh parsley, chopped
- Sea salt and ground black pepper, to taste
- 1 tsp olive oil

Instructions:
1. In a mixing bowl, thoroughly combine the turkey mince, instant oats, chopped sun-dried tomatoes, crumbled feta cheese, beaten egg, chopped onion, crushed garlic cloves, chopped parsley, sea salt, and ground black pepper.
2. Shape the mixture into 4 equal-sized patties.
3. Brush the bottom of the Air Fryer cooking basket with olive oil.
4. Place the turkey burger patties into the Air Fryer cooking basket.
5. Air fry the turkey burgers at 180 degrees Celsius for about 15 minutes, flipping them halfway through the cooking time.
6. Once cooked through and golden brown, remove the turkey burgers from the Air Fryer.
7. Serve the warm turkey burgers with toppings of your choice.
8. Enjoy your delicious homemade turkey burgers!

Nutritional Information (Per Serving): Calories: 320 / Fat: 16.7g / Carbs: 11.4g / Fiber: 2.3g / Protein: 34.3g

Chicken, Spinach & Rice Casserole

Prep time: 10 minutes / Cook time: 1 hour
Serves 4

Ingredients:
- 1/2 cup (100g) brown rice
- 1.3 lb (600g) chicken tenders
- 1 tbsp olive oil   • 1 tsp lemon zest
- 1 tbsp Italian herb mix
- 1 small red onion, thinly sliced
- 1 fat garlic clove, minced
- 1 bell pepper, thinly sliced
- 3.4 fl oz (100ml) chicken stock
- 7 oz (200g) spinach, fresh or frozen, torn into pieces
- 2 large eggs   • 3.5 oz (100g) sour cream

Instructions:
1. Cook 1/2 cup (100g) of brown rice in 200ml of water for about 30 minutes. Once cooked, add the rice to a lightly greased casserole dish.
2. In a mixing bowl, combine the chicken tenders, olive oil, lemon zest, Italian herb mix, thinly sliced red onion, minced garlic clove, thinly sliced bell pepper, chicken stock, and torn spinach pieces. Gently stir to combine.
3. Transfer the mixture to the casserole dish with the cooked brown rice.
4. Place the casserole dish in the Air Fryer and bake at 180 degrees Celsius for 15 minutes.
5. In a separate bowl, whisk the eggs with the sour cream until frothy.
6. After 15 minutes of baking, top the casserole with the egg and sour cream mixture.
7. Return the casserole dish to the Air Fryer and bake for a further 15 minutes.
8. Serve the casserole hot and enjoy!

Nutritional Information (Per Serving): Calories: 384 / Fat: 13.5g / Carbs: 26.1g / Fiber: 2.5g / Protein: 38.3g

Chapter 3: Beef, Pork, and Lamb Recipes

Pork Meatballs

Prep time: 10 minutes / Cook time: 12 minutes / Makes 18 meatballs

Ingredients:
- 454g (1 pound) ground pork
- 1 large egg, whisked
- 2.5g (1/2 teaspoon) garlic powder
- 2.5g (1/2 teaspoon) salt
- 2.5g (1/2 teaspoon) ground ginger
- 1.25g (1/4 teaspoon) crushed red pepper flakes
- 1 medium scallion, trimmed and sliced

Instructions:
1. In a large bowl, combine the ground pork, whisked egg, garlic powder, salt, ground ginger, crushed red pepper flakes, and sliced scallion.
2. Spoon out 2 tablespoons of the mixture and roll it into a ball. Repeat this process until you have formed eighteen meatballs in total.
3. Place the meatballs into the ungreased air fryer basket. Adjust the temperature to 400°F (204°C) and air fry for 12 minutes, shaking the basket three times during cooking.
4. Once done, the meatballs should be browned and have an internal temperature of at least 145°F (63°C). Serve them warm.

Nutritional Information (Per Serving): 1 meatball: Calories: 35 / Fat: 1g / Protein: 6g / Carbs: 0g / Fiber: 0g / Sodium: 86mg

Air Fryer Baby Back Ribs

**Prep time: 5 minutes / Cook time: 25 minutes
Serves 4**

Ingredients:
- 907g (2 pounds) baby back ribs
- 2 teaspoons chili powder
- 1 teaspoon paprika
- 1/2 teaspoon onion powder
- 1/2 teaspoon garlic powder
- 1/4 teaspoon ground cayenne pepper
- 120ml (1/2 cup) low-carb, sugar-free barbecue sauce

Instructions:
1. Begin by rubbing the baby back ribs with chili powder, paprika, onion powder, garlic powder, and ground cayenne pepper.
2. Place the seasoned ribs into the air fryer basket.
3. Set the air fryer temperature to 400°F (204°C) and cook for 25 minutes.
4. Once done, the ribs should appear dark and charred, with an internal temperature of at least 185°F (85°C).
5. Brush the ribs with the low-carb, sugar-free barbecue sauce and serve them warm.

Nutritional Information (Per Serving): Calories: 571 / Fat: 36g / Protein: 45g / Carbs: 17g / Fiber: 1g / Sodium: 541mg

Short Ribs with Chimichurri

Prep time: 30 minutes / Cook time: 13 minutes
Serves 4

Ingredients:
- 1 pound (454g / about 2 cups) boneless short ribs
- 1½ teaspoons sea salt, divided
- ½ teaspoon freshly ground black pepper, divided
- ½ cup (15g) fresh parsley leaves
- ½ cup (15g) fresh cilantro leaves
- 1 teaspoon minced garlic
- 1 tablespoon freshly squeezed lemon juice
- ½ teaspoon ground cumin • Avocado oil spray
- ¼ teaspoon red pepper flakes
- 2 tablespoons (30ml) extra-virgin olive oil

Instructions:
1. Begin by patting the short ribs dry with paper towels. Season them evenly with 1 teaspoon of salt and ¼ teaspoon of black pepper. Let them sit at room temperature for 45 minutes.
2. While the ribs are resting, prepare the chimichurri sauce. In a blender or food processor, combine the parsley, cilantro, minced garlic, lemon juice, ground cumin, red pepper flakes, remaining ½ teaspoon of salt, and remaining ¼ teaspoon of black pepper. With the blender running, gradually add the olive oil until the mixture becomes smooth and well combined.
3. Preheat the air fryer to 400°F (204°C). Spray both sides of the ribs with avocado oil. Place them in the air fryer basket and cook for 8 minutes. Flip the ribs and continue cooking for an additional 5 minutes, or until an instant-read thermometer registers 125°F (52°C) for medium-rare or to your desired level of doneness.
4. Allow the ribs to rest for 5 to 10 minutes before slicing. Serve them warm with the prepared chimichurri sauce.

Nutritional Information (Per Serving):Calories: 251 / Fat: 17g / Protein: 25g / Carbs: 1g / Fiber: 1g / Sodium: 651mg

Air Fryer Pork Milanese

Prep time: 10 minutes / Cook time: 12 minutes
Serves 4

Ingredients:
- 4 boneless pork chops (1-inch thick) (about 680g)
- Fine sea salt and ground black pepper, to taste
- 2 large eggs • Lemon slices, for serving
- ¾ cup powdered Parmesan cheese (75g)
- Chopped fresh parsley, for garnish

Instructions:
1. Begin by spraying the air fryer basket with avocado oil and preheating the air fryer to 400°F (204°C).
2. Place the pork chops between two sheets of plastic wrap and gently pound them with the flat side of a meat tenderizer until they reach a thickness of ¼ inch. Season both sides of the chops lightly with salt and pepper.
3. In a shallow bowl, lightly beat the eggs. Divide the powdered Parmesan cheese evenly between two bowls. Arrange the bowls in the following order: Parmesan, eggs, Parmesan. Dredge each pork chop in the first bowl of Parmesan, then dip it in the eggs, and finally dredge it again in the second bowl of Parmesan, ensuring all sides are well coated. Repeat this process for the remaining chops.
4. Place the coated pork chops in the air fryer basket and cook for 12 minutes, or until the internal temperature reaches 145°F (63°C), flipping them halfway through the cooking time.
5. Once cooked, garnish the pork Milanese with chopped fresh parsley and serve immediately with lemon slices.
6. Any leftovers can be stored in an airtight container in the refrigerator for up to 3 days. To reheat, place them in a preheated 390°F (199°C) air fryer for 5 minutes or until warmed through.

Nutritional Information (Per Serving):Calories: 349 / Fat: 14g / Protein: 50g / Carbs: 3g / Fiber: 0g / Sodium: 464mg

Air Fryer Cube Steak Roll-Ups

Prep time: 30 minutes / Cook time: 8 to 10 minutes
Serves 4

Ingredients:
- 4 cube steaks (about 24 ounces or 680 grams total)
- 1 3/4 cups (454 grams) bottled Italian dressing
- 1 teaspoon salt
- 1/2 teaspoon freshly ground black pepper
- 1/2 cup finely chopped yellow onion (120g)
- 1/2 cup finely chopped green bell pepper (120g)
- 1/2 cup finely chopped mushrooms (120g)
- 1 to 2 tablespoons oil

Instructions:
1. Place the cube steaks in a large resealable bag or airtight container and pour the Italian dressing over them. Seal the bag or container and refrigerate for 2 hours to marinate.
2. After marinating, remove the steaks from the bag and discard the marinade. Season the steaks evenly with salt and pepper.
3. In a small bowl, mix together the chopped onion, green bell pepper, and mushrooms. Spread this mixture evenly over the steaks.
4. Roll up each steak jelly-roll style and secure them with toothpicks.
5. Preheat your air fryer to 400°F (204°C).
6. Place the steak roll-ups in the air fryer basket and cook for 4 minutes. Then, flip the roll-ups, spritz them with oil, and cook for an additional 4 to 6 minutes, or until the internal temperature reaches 145°F (63°C).
7. Allow the roll-ups to rest for 5 minutes before serving.

*Nutritional Information (Per Serving):*Calories: 364 / Fat: 20g / Protein: 37g / Carbs: 7g / Fiber: 1g / Sodium: 715mg

Spicy Lamb Sirloin Chops

Prep time: 30 minutes / Cook time: 15 minutes
Serves 4

Ingredients:
- 1/2 yellow onion, coarsely chopped
- 4 coin-size slices peeled fresh ginger
- 5 garlic cloves   • 1 teaspoon garam masala
- 1 teaspoon ground fennel
- 1 teaspoon ground cinnamon
- 1 teaspoon ground turmeric
- 1/2 to 1 teaspoon cayenne pepper
- 1/2 teaspoon ground cardamom
- 1 teaspoon kosher salt
- 454g (1 pound) lamb sirloin chops

Instructions:
1. In a blender, combine the chopped onion, ginger slices, garlic cloves, garam masala, ground fennel, ground cinnamon, ground turmeric, cayenne pepper, ground cardamom, and kosher salt. Pulse until the mixture forms a thick paste, about 3 to 4 minutes.
2. Place the lamb chops in a large bowl. Using a sharp knife, make several slashes on both sides of the meat and fat to allow the marinade to penetrate. Add the spice paste to the bowl and toss the lamb chops until evenly coated. Marinate at room temperature for 30 minutes or refrigerate for up to 24 hours.
3. Preheat the air fryer to 325°F (163°C). Place the marinated lamb chops in a single layer in the air fryer basket. Cook for 15 minutes, flipping the chops halfway through the cooking time, until they reach an internal temperature of 145°F (63°C) for medium-rare.
4. Serve the spicy lamb sirloin chops hot, garnished with fresh herbs if desired.

*Nutritional Information (Per Serving):*Calories: 179 / Fat: 7g / Protein: 24g / Carbs: 4g / Fiber: 1g / Sodium: 657mg

Air Fryer Kheema Meatloaf

Prep time: 10 minutes / Cook time: 15 minutes
Serves 4

Ingredients:
- 454g (about 2 cups) 85% lean ground beef
- 2 large eggs, lightly beaten
- 150g (about 1 cup) diced yellow onion
- 60g (about 1/4 cup) chopped fresh cilantro
- 15g (about 1 tablespoon) minced fresh ginger
- 15g (about 1 tablespoon) minced garlic
- 5g (about 2 teaspoons) garam masala
- 5g (about 1 teaspoon) kosher salt
- 5g (about 1 teaspoon) ground turmeric
- 2.5g (about 1/2 teaspoon) cayenne pepper
- 2.5g (about 1/2 teaspoon) ground cinnamon
- 0.5g (about 1/8 teaspoon) ground cardamom

Instructions:
1. In a large bowl, combine the 85% lean ground beef, lightly beaten eggs, diced yellow onion, chopped fresh cilantro, minced fresh ginger, minced garlic, garam masala, kosher salt, ground turmeric, cayenne pepper, ground cinnamon, and ground cardamom. Mix gently until thoroughly combined.
2. Transfer the seasoned meat mixture into a baking pan and place the pan in the air fryer basket.
3. Set the air fryer to 350°F (177°C) and cook for 15 minutes or until the internal temperature of the meatloaf reaches 160°F (71°C).
4. Once cooked, drain any excess fat and liquid from the pan and let the meatloaf stand for 5 minutes before slicing.
5. Slice the meatloaf and serve hot.

Nutritional Information (Per Serving): Calories: 205 / Fat: 8g / Protein: 28g / Carbs: 5g / Fiber: 1g / Sodium: 696mg

Cajun Blackened Pork Roast

Prep time: 20 minutes / Cook time: 33 minutes
Serves 4

Ingredients:
- 907g (2 pounds) bone-in pork loin roast
- 2 tablespoons oil
- 1/4 cup Cajun seasoning (about 60g)
- 1/2 cup diced onion (about 75g)
- 1/2 cup diced celery (about 60g)
- 1/2 cup diced green bell pepper (about 75g)
- 1 tablespoon minced garlic (about 12g)

Instructions:
1. Begin by making 5 slits across the pork roast. Spritz the roast with oil, ensuring it's completely coated. Evenly sprinkle the Cajun seasoning over the pork roast.
2. In a medium bowl, combine the diced onion, celery, green bell pepper, and minced garlic. Set the mixture aside.
3. Preheat your air fryer to 360°F (182°C) and line the basket with parchment paper.
4. Place the pork roast on the parchment paper and spritz it with oil.
5. Cook for 5 minutes, then flip the roast and cook for an additional 5 minutes. Repeat this process in 5-minute intervals until the total cook time reaches 20 minutes.
6. Increase the air fryer temperature to 390°F (199°C).
7. Continue cooking the roast for 8 more minutes, then flip it. Add the vegetable mixture to the basket and cook for a final 5 minutes.
8. Allow the roast to rest for 5 minutes before serving.

Nutritional Information (Per Serving): Calories: 400 / Fat: 16g / Protein: 52g / Carbs: 8g / Fiber: 2g / Sodium: 738mg

Tangy Beef Strips

Prep time: 30 minutes / Cook time: 14 minutes
Serves 4

Ingredients:
- 680g (1½ pounds) sirloin steak
- 60ml (1/4 cup) red wine
- 60ml (1/4 cup) fresh lime juice
- 1 teaspoon garlic powder
- 1 teaspoon shallot powder
- 1 teaspoon celery seeds
- 1 teaspoon mustard seeds
- Coarse sea salt and ground black pepper, to taste
- 1 teaspoon red pepper flakes
- 2 eggs, lightly whisked
- 100g (1 cup) Parmesan cheese • 1 teaspoon paprika

Instructions:
1. In a large ceramic bowl, combine the sirloin steak, red wine, lime juice, garlic powder, shallot powder, celery seeds, mustard seeds, salt, black pepper, and red pepper flakes. Allow it to marinate for 3 hours.
2. After marinating, tenderize the steak by pounding it with a mallet, then cut it into 1-inch strips.
3. Whisk the eggs in a shallow bowl. In another bowl, mix the Parmesan cheese and paprika.
4. Dip each beef strip into the whisked eggs, ensuring it's coated on all sides. Then, dredge the beef strips in the Parmesan mixture.
5. Cook the beef strips in the air fryer at 400°F (204°C) for 14 minutes, flipping them halfway through.
6. While the beef is cooking, heat the reserved marinade in a saucepan over medium heat until it simmers.
7. Serve the cooked steak strips with the warmed marinade sauce on the side. Enjoy!

*Nutritional Information (Per Serving):*Calories: 483 / Fat: 29g / Protein: 49g / Carbs: 4g / Fiber: 1g / Sodium: 141mg

Parmesan-Coated Pork Cutlets

Prep time: 5 minutes / Cook time: 12 minutes
Serves 4

Ingredients:
- 1 large egg
- 120g (1/2 cup) grated Parmesan cheese
- 4 boneless pork chops (113g / 4 ounces each)
- 1/2 teaspoon salt
- 1/4 teaspoon ground black pepper

Instructions:
1. In a medium bowl, whisk the egg. In a separate medium bowl, place the grated Parmesan cheese.
2. Season both sides of the pork chops with salt and pepper. Dip each pork chop into the whisked egg, then coat both sides with Parmesan cheese.
3. Arrange the pork chops in the air fryer basket. Set the temperature to 400°F (204°C) and air fry for 12 minutes, flipping the chops halfway through cooking.
4. Once done, the pork chops should be golden and reach an internal temperature of at least 145°F (63°C). Serve hot.

*Nutritional Information (Per Serving):*Calories: 218 / Fat: 9g / Protein: 32g / Carbs: 1g / Fiber: 0g / Sodium: 372mg

Spicy Beef Shreds

Prep time: 5 minutes / Cook time: 35 minutes
Serves 6

Ingredients:

- 907g (2 pounds) beef chuck roast, cut into 2-inch cubes
- 1 teaspoon salt
- 1/2 teaspoon ground black pepper
- 120ml (1/2 cup) no-sugar-added chipotle sauce

Instructions:

1. In a large bowl, season beef cubes with salt and pepper, ensuring they are evenly coated. Place the seasoned beef into the air fryer basket. Set the temperature to 400°F (204°C) and air fry for 30 minutes, shaking the basket halfway through cooking. Check the internal temperature of the beef, ensuring it reaches at least 160°F (71°C) to ensure doneness.
2. Transfer the cooked beef to a large bowl and shred it using two forks. Pour in the chipotle sauce and toss until the beef is evenly coated.
3. Return the shredded beef to the air fryer basket and air fry for an additional 5 minutes at 400°F (204°C) to crisp up with the sauce. Serve the spicy beef shreds warm.

*Nutritional Information (Per Serving):*Calories: 204 / Fat: 9g / Protein: 31g / Carbs: 0g / Fiber: 0g / Sodium: 539mg

Herbed Mushroom Sirloin Bites

Prep time: 30 minutes / Cook time: 10 minutes
Serves 4

Ingredients:

- 680g (1.5 pounds) sirloin, trimmed and cut into 1-inch pieces
- 227g (8 ounces) brown mushrooms, halved
- 60ml (1/4 cup) Worcestershire sauce
- 15g (1 tablespoon) Dijon mustard
- 15ml (1 tablespoon) olive oil
- 1 teaspoon paprika
- 1 teaspoon crushed red pepper flakes
- 2 tablespoons chopped fresh parsley (optional)

Instructions:

1. Combine the beef and mushrooms in a gallon-size resealable bag. In a small bowl, whisk together Worcestershire sauce, mustard, olive oil, paprika, and red pepper flakes. Pour the marinade into the bag, ensuring the beef and mushrooms are evenly coated. Seal the bag and refrigerate for at least 4 hours, preferably overnight. Remove from the refrigerator 30 minutes before cooking.
2. Preheat your air fryer to 400°F (204°C).
3. Drain and discard the marinade. Arrange the steak and mushrooms in the air fryer basket. Air fry for 10 minutes, pausing halfway through to shake the basket. Once done, transfer to a serving plate and garnish with parsley, if desired.

*Nutritional Information (Per Serving):*Calories: 383 / Fat: 23g / Protein: 37g / Carbs: 7g / Fiber: 1g / Sodium: 307mg

Chapter 4: Fish and Seafood Recipes

Spiced Salmon

Prep time: 10 minutes / Cook time: 8 minutes
Serves 2

Ingredients:
- 283g (10 ounces) salmon fillet
- 1/2 teaspoon ground coriander
- 1 teaspoon ground cumin
- 1 teaspoon dried basil
- 15ml (1 tablespoon) avocado oil

Instructions:
1. In a shallow bowl, combine the ground coriander, ground cumin, and dried basil.
2. Coat the salmon fillet evenly with the spice mixture, then drizzle with avocado oil.
3. Place the seasoned salmon fillet in the air fryer basket and cook at 395ºF (202ºC) for 4 minutes on each side.

*Nutritional Information (Per Serving):*Calories: 249 / Fat: 13g / Protein: 29g / Carbs: 1g / Fiber: 1g / Sodium: 109mg

Balsamic Tilapia

Prep time: 5 minutes / Cook time: 15 minutes
Serves 4

Ingredients:
- 680g (4 fillets) boneless tilapia
- 30ml (2 tablespoons) balsamic vinegar
- 5ml (1 teaspoon) avocado oil
- 1 teaspoon dried basil

Instructions:
1. Season the tilapia fillets with balsamic vinegar, avocado oil, and dried basil.
2. Place the seasoned fillets in the air fryer basket and cook at 365ºF (185ºC) for 15 minutes.

*Nutritional Information (Per Serving):*Calories: 129 / Fat: 3g / Protein: 23g / Carbs: 1g / Fiber: 0g / Sodium: 92mg

Salmon and Cucumber Salad

Prep time: 10 minutes / Cook time: 8 to 10 minutes
Serves 2

Ingredients:
- 454g (1 pound) salmon fillet
- 22.5ml (1 1/2 tablespoons) olive oil, divided
- 15ml (1 tablespoon) sherry vinegar
- 15ml (1 tablespoon) capers, rinsed and drained
- 1 seedless cucumber, thinly sliced
- ¼ Vidalia onion, thinly sliced
- 2 tablespoons chopped fresh parsley
- Salt and freshly ground black pepper, to taste

Instructions:
1. Preheat your air fryer to 400ºF (204ºC).
2. Coat the salmon with ½ tablespoon of olive oil. Place it skin-side down in the air fryer basket and cook for 8 to 10 minutes until it's opaque and flakes easily with a fork. Once done, transfer the salmon to a plate and allow it to cool to room temperature. Remove the skin and gently flake the fish into bite-size pieces.
3. In a small bowl, whisk together the remaining 1 tablespoon of olive oil and the sherry vinegar until well combined. Add the flaked salmon, capers, cucumber, onion, and parsley. Season with salt and freshly ground black pepper according to taste. Gently toss to coat.
4. Serve immediately or refrigerate for up to 4 hours before serving.

*Nutritional Information (Per Serving):*Calories: 399 / Fat: 20g / Protein: 47g / Carbs: 4g / Fiber: 1g / Sodium: 276mg

Spicy Flounder Cutlets

Prep time: 15 minutes / Cook time: 10 minutes
Serves 2

Ingredients:
- 1 egg
- 100g (about 1 cup) Pecorino Romano cheese, grated
- Sea salt and white pepper, to taste
- 2.5g (about 1/2 teaspoon) cayenne pepper
- 1 teaspoon dried parsley flakes
- 2 flounder fillets

Instructions:
1. Begin by whisking the egg until it becomes frothy to prepare the breading station.
2. In a separate bowl, combine the Pecorino Romano cheese with the spices.
3. Dip each flounder fillet in the egg mixture, ensuring it's evenly coated. Then, dredge the fillets in the cheese and spice mixture, ensuring they're coated evenly on both sides.
4. Preheat your air fryer to 390ºF (199ºC). Place the coated flounder fillets in the air fryer basket and cook for 5 minutes. Flip them over and cook for an additional 5 minutes until they are golden brown and crispy.
5. Serve the flounder cutlets immediately and enjoy!

*Nutritional Information (Per Serving):*Calories: 280 / Fat: 13g / Protein: 36g / Carbs: 3g / Fiber: 1g / Sodium: 257mg

Zesty Lemon Mahi-Mahi

**Prep time: 5 minutes / Cook time: 14 minutes
Serves 2**

Ingredients:
- Oil, for spraying
- 340g (2 fillets, about 6 ounces each) mahi-mahi
- 15ml (1 tablespoon) lemon juice
- 15ml (1 tablespoon) olive oil
- 1.25g (1/4 teaspoon) salt
- 0.6g (1/4 teaspoon) freshly ground black pepper
- 1 tablespoon chopped fresh dill
- 2 lemon slices

Instructions:
1. Lightly spray oil on the air fryer basket and line it with parchment paper.
2. Place the mahi-mahi fillets in the prepared basket.
3. In a small bowl, whisk together lemon juice and olive oil. Brush the mixture evenly over the mahi-mahi fillets.
4. Sprinkle salt and black pepper over the mahi-mahi, then top with chopped dill.
5. Air fry at 400ºF (204ºC) for 12 to 14 minutes, depending on the thickness of the fillets, until they flake easily.
6. Serve the cooked mahi-mahi on plates, each topped with a lemon slice.

Nutritional Information (Per Serving): Calories: 218 / Fat: 8g / Protein: 32g / Carbs: 3g / Fiber: 1g / Sodium: 441mg

Crispy Shrimp Tacos

**Prep time: 10 minutes / Cook time: 9 minutes /
Makes 8 tacos**

Ingredients:
- 454g (1 pound) small shrimp, peeled, deveined, and tails removed   • 2 large eggs
- 1 teaspoon prepared yellow mustard
- 120g (1/2 cup) finely shredded Gouda or Parmesan cheese   • 120g (1/2 cup) pork dust
- 60g (1/4 cup) pico de gallo • 8 large Boston lettuce leaves
- 60g (1/4 cup) shredded purple cabbage
- 1 lemon, sliced   • Guacamole (optional)

Instructions:
1. Preheat the air fryer to 400ºF (204ºC).
2. In a large bowl, whisk together the eggs and mustard until well combined. Add the shrimp and toss to coat.
3. In a separate medium-sized bowl, mix the cheese and pork dust until thoroughly combined.
4. Roll each shrimp in the cheese and pork dust mixture, ensuring they are evenly coated. Press the mixture onto each shrimp using your hands.
5. Spray the coated shrimp with avocado oil and arrange them in the air fryer basket, leaving space between each shrimp.
6. Air fry the shrimp for 9 minutes, flipping halfway through, until they are cooked through and golden brown.
7. To serve, place a lettuce leaf on a plate, add several shrimp on top, and sprinkle with pico de gallo and purple cabbage. Squeeze lemon juice over the tacos and serve with guacamole, if desired.
8. Store any leftover shrimp in an airtight container in the refrigerator for up to 3 days. Reheat in a preheated 400ºF (204ºC) air fryer for 5 minutes or until warmed through.

Nutritional Information (Per Serving): Calories: 115 / Fat: 4g / Protein: 18g / Carbs: 2g / Fiber: 1g / Sodium: 253mg

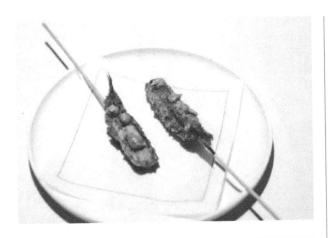

Grilled Swordfish Skewers

Prep time: 30 minutes / Cook time: 6 to 8 minutes
Serves 4

Ingredients:
- 454g (1 pound) filleted swordfish, cut into 1½-inch chunks
- 60ml (1/4 cup) avocado oil
- 30ml (2 tablespoons) freshly squeezed lemon juice
- 15g (1 tablespoon) minced fresh parsley
- 10g (2 teaspoons) Dijon mustard
- Sea salt and freshly ground black pepper, to taste
- 85g (3 ounces) cherry tomatoes

Instructions:
1. Cut the swordfish into 1½-inch chunks, ensuring to remove any remaining bones.
2. In a large bowl, whisk together the avocado oil, lemon juice, parsley, and Dijon mustard. Season with salt and pepper to taste. Add the swordfish chunks to the bowl and toss until they are evenly coated with the marinade. Cover the bowl and refrigerate for 30 minutes to marinate.
3. After marinating, remove the swordfish from the bowl. Thread the marinated swordfish and cherry tomatoes onto 4 skewers, alternating them as you go.
4. Preheat the air fryer to 400°F (204°C). Place the skewers in the air fryer basket and cook for 3 minutes. Flip the skewers and continue cooking for an additional 3 to 5 minutes until the swordfish is cooked through and reaches an internal temperature of 140°F (60°C) when tested with an instant-read thermometer.

Nutritional Information (Per Serving): Calories: 291 / Fat: 21g / Protein: 23g / Carbs: 2g / Fiber: 0g / Sodium: 121mg

Herb-infused Snapper En Papillote

Prep time: 20 minutes / Cook time: 15 minutes
Serves 2

Ingredients:
- 2 snapper fillets
- 1 shallot, thinly sliced
- 2 garlic cloves, halved
- 1 bell pepper, thinly sliced
- 1 small-sized serrano pepper, thinly sliced
- 1 tomato, thinly sliced
- 15ml (1 tablespoon) olive oil
- 1g (¼ teaspoon) freshly ground black pepper
- 2.5g (½ teaspoon) paprika
- Sea salt, to taste
- 2 bay leaves

Instructions:
1. Lay out two parchment sheets on your working surface. Place each fish fillet in the center of one side of the parchment paper.
2. Arrange the shallot, garlic, bell pepper, serrano pepper, and tomato slices over the fish. Drizzle olive oil evenly over the fish and vegetables. Season with black pepper, paprika, and salt. Place a bay leaf on top of each fillet.
3. Fold the other half of the parchment paper over the fish to cover it completely, then tightly fold and crimp the edges to seal the package, creating a half-moon shape.
4. Preheat your air fryer to 390°F (199°C). Once heated, place the parchment packets in the air fryer basket and cook for 15 minutes.
5. Carefully remove the packets from the air fryer. Open them carefully to avoid steam burns. Serve the snapper and vegetables warm directly from the parchment.

Nutritional Information (Per Serving): Calories: 325 / Fat: 10g / Protein: 47g / Carbs: 11g / Fiber: 2g / Sodium: 146mg

Crispy-Coated Catfish Delight

Prep time: 10 minutes / Cook time: 12 minutes
Serves 4

Ingredients:
- 4 catfish fillets (7 ounces / 198 g each)
- 80ml (⅓ cup) heavy whipping cream
- 15ml (1 tablespoon) lemon juice
- 112g (1 cup) blanched finely ground almond flour
- 2 teaspoons Old Bay seasoning
- 2.5g (½ teaspoon) salt
- 0.6g (¼ teaspoon) ground black pepper

Instructions:
1. In a large bowl, combine the catfish fillets with heavy whipping cream and lemon juice, ensuring they are evenly coated.
2. In another large bowl, mix the almond flour and Old Bay seasoning.
3. Remove each fillet from the cream mixture and shake off any excess. Season with salt and pepper.
4. Press each fillet into the almond flour mixture, coating both sides evenly.
5. Place the coated fillets into the air fryer basket. Set the temperature to 400ºF (204ºC) and air fry for 12 minutes, flipping the fillets halfway through cooking.
6. Once done, the catfish should be golden brown and have reached an internal temperature of at least 145ºF (63ºC). Serve warm.

*Nutritional Information (Per Serving):*Calories: 438 / Fat: 28g / Protein: 41g / Carbs: 7g / Fiber: 4g / Sodium: 387mg

Speedy Shrimp Skewers

Prep time: 10 minutes / Cook time: 5 minutes
Serves 5

Ingredients:
- 1.8 kg (4 pounds) shrimp, peeled
- 15g (1 tablespoon) dried rosemary
- 15ml (1 tablespoon) avocado oil
- 5ml (1 teaspoon) apple cider vinegar

Instructions:
1. In a large bowl, toss the peeled shrimp with dried rosemary, avocado oil, and apple cider vinegar until well coated.
2. Thread the seasoned shrimp onto skewers and arrange them in the air fryer basket.
3. Air fry the shrimp at 400ºF (204ºC) for 5 minutes.
4. Once cooked, serve the shrimp skewers immediately.

*Nutritional Information (Per Serving):*Calories: 336 / Fat: 5g / Protein: 73g / Carbs: 0g / Fiber: 0g / Sodium: 432mg

Apple Cider Mussels

Prep time: 10 minutes / Cook time: 2 minutes
Serves 5

Ingredients:
- 907g (2 pounds) mussels, cleaned and peeled
- 1 teaspoon onion powder
- 1 teaspoon ground cumin
- 15ml (1 tablespoon) avocado oil
- 60ml (1/4 cup) apple cider vinegar

Instructions:
1. In a bowl, combine the cleaned mussels with onion powder, ground cumin, avocado oil, and apple cider vinegar, ensuring the mussels are evenly coated.
2. Transfer the seasoned mussels to the air fryer and cook at 395°F (202°C) for 2 minutes.
3. Once cooked, serve the apple cider mussels immediately.

*Nutritional Information (Per Serving):*Calories: 187 / Fat: 7g / Protein: 22g / Carbs: 7g / Fiber: 0g / Sodium: 521mg

Everything Bagel Ahi Tuna Steaks

Prep time: 5 minutes / Cook time: 14 minutes
Serves 2

Ingredients:
- 340g (2 pieces, 6 ounces each) ahi tuna steaks
- 30ml (2 tablespoons) olive oil
- 3 tablespoons everything bagel seasoning

Instructions:
1. Begin by drizzling both sides of each tuna steak with olive oil. On a medium plate, spread out the everything bagel seasoning. Press each side of the tuna steaks into the seasoning to form a thick layer.
2. Place the seasoned tuna steaks into the ungreased air fryer basket. Set the temperature to 400°F (204°C) and air fry for 14 minutes, ensuring to turn the steaks halfway through cooking. The steaks will be done when the internal temperature reaches at least 145°F (63°C) for well-done. Serve the tuna steaks warm.

*Nutritional Information (Per Serving):*Calories: 305 / Fat: 14g / Protein: 42g / Carbs: 0g / Fiber: 0g / Sodium: 377mg

Garlic Rosemary Prawns

Prep time: 10 minutes / Cook time: 12 minutes
Serves 4

Ingredients:
- 21.2 oz (600g) tiger prawns, peeled and deveined
- 2 fat garlic cloves, crushed
- 1 tbsp dried rosemary, crushed
- 1 tbsp lemon juice
- 1 tbsp olive oil

Instructions:
1. Preheat your Air Fryer to 200 degrees C.
2. In a bowl, toss the peeled and deveined tiger prawns with crushed garlic cloves, crushed dried rosemary, lemon juice, and olive oil until they are well coated.
3. Lightly brush the prawns with any remaining mixture.
4. Lower the seasoned prawns into the lightly oiled cooking basket of the Air Fryer.
5. Cook the prawns in the preheated Air Fryer for 12 minutes, shaking the basket halfway through the cooking time to ensure even browning.
6. Once cooked, serve the garlic rosemary prawns warm and enjoy!

*Nutritional Information (Per Serving):*Calories: 171 / Fat: 5.4g / Carbs: 2.6g / Fiber: 0.1g / Protein: 26.2g

Cod and Potato Traybake

Prep time: 10 minutes / Cook time: 27 minutes
Serves 4

Ingredients:
- 4 fat garlic cloves, smashed
- 1 tsp dried rosemary
- Coarse sea salt and ground black pepper, to taste
- 1 tbsp olive oil
- 21.2 oz (600g) cod fillets
- 14.1 oz (400g) potatoes, peeled and cut into wedges

Instructions:
1. Preheat your Air Fryer to 190 degrees C.
2. Crush the smashed garlic cloves and dried rosemary using a mortar and pestle. Add coarse sea salt, ground black pepper, and olive oil. Stir the mixture to combine.
3. In a large bowl, toss the cod fillets and potato wedges with the freshly prepared garlic and rosemary mixture until they are evenly coated.
4. Lower the seasoned potato wedges into a parchment-lined baking tin.
5. Place the baking tin into the cooking basket of the Air Fryer and bake the potatoes for 15 minutes.
6. After 15 minutes, remove the baking tin from the Air Fryer and add the cod fillets.
7. Return the baking tin to the Air Fryer and continue to bake for a further 12 minutes, or until the fish is opaque and the potatoes are thoroughly cooked.
8. Once cooked, serve the tuna and potatoes in the tin.
9. Enjoy your delicious tuna and potato traybake!

*Nutritional Information (Per Serving):*Calories: 234 / Fat: 4.4g / Carbs: 17.9g / Fiber: 2g / Protein: 29g

Peppery Scallops

Prep time: 10 minutes / Cook time: 8 minutes
Serves 3

Ingredients:
- 21.2 oz (600g) sea scallops
- 1 tbsp whole peppercorns, cracked
- 1 fat garlic clove, peeled
- 1 small lemon, freshly squeezed
- 1 tsp olive oil
- 1 tsp mustard seeds
- 1 sprig thyme
- Coarse sea salt, to taste

Instructions:
1. Preheat your Air Fryer to 200 degrees C.
2. Rub the sea scallops with the cracked whole peppercorns, peeled fat garlic clove, freshly squeezed lemon juice, olive oil, mustard seeds, thyme sprig, and coarse sea salt until they are evenly coated.
3. Arrange the seasoned scallops in the cooking basket of the Air Fryer.
4. Air fry the scallops at 200 degrees C for 8 minutes, shaking the basket halfway through the cooking time to promote even cooking.
5. Once cooked, remove the scallops from the Air Fryer and serve them with a fresh Mediterranean salad of your choice.
6. Enjoy your peppery scallops!

Nutritional Information (Per Serving): Calories: 188 / Fat: 5.6g / Carbs: 8.2g / Fiber: 0.2g / Protein: 24.2g

Sweet Potato Crab Cakes

Prep time: 10 minutes / Cook time: 34 minutes
Serves 4

Ingredients:
- 14.1 oz (400g) sweet potatoes, peeled and diced
- 1 tbsp olive oil   • 1.8 oz (50g) oat flour
- Sea salt and ground black pepper, to taste
- 1 tsp mustard powder   • 1 fat garlic clove, minced
- 1 large red onion, finely chopped
- 7 oz (200g) crabmeat   • A pinch of Aleppo pepper
- 1 medium egg, lightly beaten
- 3.5 oz (100g) breadcrumbs

Instructions:
1. Preheat your Air Fryer to 190 degrees C.
2. In a bowl, toss the diced sweet potatoes with 1 teaspoon of olive oil, sea salt, and ground black pepper until they are evenly coated.
3. Place the seasoned sweet potatoes in the Air Fryer cooking basket and cook for about 20 minutes, shaking the basket halfway through cooking, until they are just tender.
4. Once cooked, mash the sweet potatoes in a mixing bowl.
5. Stir in the mustard powder, minced garlic clove, finely chopped red onion, crabmeat, Aleppo pepper, oat flour, and lightly beaten egg until well combined.
6. Shape the mixture into patties.
7. Lightly oil the Air Fryer cooking basket and lower the crab cakes into it.
8. Air fry the crab cakes at 180 degrees C for about 14 minutes, until they are cooked through and golden brown.
9. Serve the sweet potato crab cakes and enjoy!

Nutritional Information (Per Serving): Calories: 303 / Fat: 7.6g / Carbs: 43.3g / Fiber: 4.9g / Protein: 16.5g

Cauliflower and Tuna Vegetable Patties

Prep time: 10 minutes / Cook time: 14 minutes
Serves 4

Ingredients:
- 7.1 oz (200g) cauliflower, grated
- 7.1 oz (200g) carrots, grated
- 1 (185g) can tuna, canned in water, flaked
- 1 tbsp olive oil
- 1 small leek, chopped
- 3.5 oz (100g) plain flour
- 1 medium egg, beaten
- 3.5 oz (100g) instant oats
- 1 tsp red pepper flakes
- Coarse sea salt and ground black pepper, to taste

Instructions:
1. Preheat your Air Fryer to 180 degrees C.
2. In a bowl, mix together the grated cauliflower, grated carrots, flaked tuna, chopped leek, plain flour, beaten egg, instant oats, red pepper flakes, coarse sea salt, and ground black pepper until well combined.
3. Shape the mixture into small patties.
4. Lightly oil the Air Fryer cooking basket and place the patties in it.
5. Flatten the patties slightly using a fork and brush them with olive oil.
6. Cook the patties in the Air Fryer at 180 degrees C for about 14 minutes, or until they are cooked through and golden brown.
7. Once cooked, serve the cauliflower and tuna vegetable patties.
8. Enjoy your delicious meal!

*Nutritional Information (Per Serving):*Calories: 339 / Fat: 7.5g / Carbs: 47.1g / Fiber: 6.3g / Protein: 22.3g

Chapter 5: Snacks and Appetizer Recipes

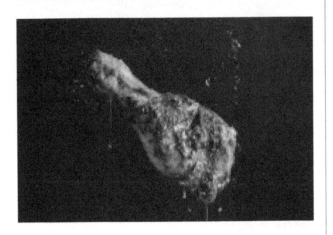

Lemon-Pepper Chicken Drumsticks

Prep time: 30 minutes / Cook time: 30 minutes
Serves 2

Ingredients:
- 8 teaspoons freshly ground coarse black pepper
- 2 teaspoons baking powder
- 1 teaspoon garlic powder
- 4 chicken drumsticks (113 g each)
- Kosher salt, to taste
- 1 lemon

Instructions:
1. In a small bowl, combine the freshly ground black pepper, baking powder, and garlic powder. Place the chicken drumsticks on a plate and evenly sprinkle them with the mixture, ensuring they are well coated. Allow the drumsticks to marinate in the refrigerator for at least 1 hour or overnight.
2. Sprinkle the drumsticks with kosher salt. Transfer them to the air fryer basket, positioning them bone-end up against the wall of the basket. Air fry at 375ºF (191ºC) until the drumsticks are cooked through and crispy on the outside, approximately 30 minutes.
3. Once cooked, transfer the drumsticks to a serving platter. Grate the zest of the lemon over the hot drumsticks. Cut the lemon into wedges and serve alongside the warm drumsticks.

Nutritional Information (Per Serving): Calories: 438 / Fat: 24g / Protein: 48g / Carbs: 6g / Fiber: 2g / Sodium: 279mg

Turkey Burger Sliders

Prep time: 10 minutes / Cook time: 5 to 7 minutes /
Makes 8 sliders

Ingredients:
- 454g (1 pound) ground turkey
- 1/4 teaspoon curry powder
- 1 teaspoon Hoisin sauce
- 1/2 teaspoon salt
- 8 slider buns
- 60g (1/2 cup) slivered red onions
- 60g (1/2 cup) slivered green or red bell pepper
- 60g (1/2 cup) fresh chopped pineapple
- Light cream cheese, softened

Instructions:
1. In a mixing bowl, combine the ground turkey, curry powder, Hoisin sauce, and salt, and mix thoroughly.
2. Shape the turkey mixture into 8 small patties.
3. Place the patties in the air fryer basket and cook at 360ºF (182ºC) for 5 to 7 minutes until they are well done and the juices run clear.
4. On each slider bun bottom, place a cooked patty and top it with slivered onions, peppers, and chopped pineapple. Spread the remaining bun halves with softened cream cheese to taste, then place them on top of the sliders.
5. Serve and enjoy!

Nutritional Information (Per Serving): 1 slider: Calories: 305 / Fat: 17g / Protein: 3g / Carbs: 34g / Fiber: 1g / Sodium: 355mg

Mexican Potato Skins

Prep time: 10 minutes / Cook time: 55 minutes
Serves 6

Ingredients:
- Olive oil   • 1 tablespoon taco seasoning
- 6 medium russet potatoes (about 900g or 6 cups), scrubbed
- Salt and freshly ground black pepper, to taste
- 240g (1 cup) fat-free refried black beans
- 120g (1/2 cup) salsa
- 85g (3/4 cup) reduced-fat shredded Cheddar cheese

Instructions:
1. Lightly spray the air fryer basket with olive oil.
2. Coat the potatoes lightly with oil and season them with salt and pepper. Use a fork to pierce each potato a few times.
3. Arrange the potatoes in the air fryer basket. Air fry at 400ºF (204ºC) until fork-tender, approximately 30 to 40 minutes, depending on their size. Note that microwaving or baking won't achieve the same crispy skin as air frying.
4. While the potatoes cook, mix the refried black beans and taco seasoning in a small bowl. Set aside until the potatoes are cool.
5. Once the potatoes are done, cut them in half lengthwise and scoop out most of the insides, leaving about ¼ inch of potato in the skins to maintain their shape.
6. Season the insides of the potato skins with salt and pepper. Lightly spray the insides with oil. You may need to air fry them in batches.
7. Place the potato skins in the air fryer basket, skin-side down, and air fry until they become crisp and golden, around 8 to 10 minutes.
8. Transfer the skins to a work surface and fill each one with ½ tablespoon of the seasoned refried black beans, 2 teaspoons salsa, and 1 tablespoon shredded Cheddar cheese.
9. Arrange the filled potato skins in the air fryer basket in a single layer. Lightly spray with oil.
10. Air fry until the cheese is melted and bubbly, for about 2 to 3 minutes.

Nutritional Information (Per Serving):Calories: 239 / Fat: 2g / Protein: 10g / Carbs: 46g / Fiber: 5g / Sodium: 492mg

Asian Five-Spice Wings

Prep time: 30 minutes / Cook time: 13 to 15 minutes
Serves 4

Ingredients:
- 907g (2 pounds) chicken wings
- 120ml (1/2 cup) Asian-style salad dressing
- 30g (2 tablespoons) Chinese five-spice powder

Instructions:
1. Begin by removing and discarding the wing tips, then cut the remaining wing pieces in half at the joint.
2. Place the wing pieces in a large sealable plastic bag. Add the Asian dressing to the bag, seal it, and massage the marinade into the wings until they are evenly coated. Refrigerate for at least an hour.
3. After marinating, remove the wings from the bag, allowing excess marinade to drain off, and transfer them to the air fryer basket.
4. Air fry the wings at 360ºF (182ºC) for 13 to 15 minutes, or until the juices run clear. Halfway through cooking, shake the basket or stir the wings to ensure even cooking.
5. Once the wings are cooked, transfer them to a plate in a single layer. Sprinkle half of the Chinese five-spice powder over the wings, turn them, and sprinkle the remaining seasoning on the other side.

Nutritional Information (Per Serving):Calories: 357 / Fat: 12g / Protein: 51g / Carbs: 9g / Fiber: 2g / Sodium: 591mg

Eggplant Fries

Prep time: 10 minutes / Cook time: 7 to 8 minutes
Serves 4

Ingredients:
- 1 medium eggplant
- 1 teaspoon cumin
- ½ teaspoon salt
- 1 teaspoon ground coriander
- 1 teaspoon garlic powder
- 1 large egg
- 120g (1 cup) crushed panko bread crumbs
- 30ml (2 tablespoons) water
- Oil for misting or cooking spray

Instructions:
1. Begin by peeling the eggplant and cutting it into fries, about ⅜- to ½-inch thick.
2. Preheat your air fryer to 390ºF (199ºC).
3. In a small cup, mix together the ground coriander, cumin, garlic powder, and salt.
4. Combine 1 teaspoon of the seasoning mix with the panko crumbs in a shallow dish.
5. Place the eggplant fries in a large bowl, sprinkle them with the remaining seasoning mix, and stir well to ensure they are evenly coated.
6. Beat the eggs and water together, then pour the mixture over the eggplant fries. Stir until the fries are coated.
7. Remove the eggplant fries from the egg wash, allowing any excess to drip off, and then roll them in the panko crumbs.
8. Spray the fries lightly with oil.
9. Place half of the fries in the air fryer basket, ensuring they are in a single layer, even if they overlap slightly.
10. Cook the fries for 5 minutes, then shake the basket, mist lightly with oil, and continue cooking for an additional 2 to 3 minutes, or until they are browned and crispy.
11. Repeat step 10 to cook the remaining eggplant fries.

Nutritional Information (Per Serving): Calories: 163 / Fat: 3g / Protein: 7g / Carbs: 28g / Fiber: 6g / Sodium: 510mg

Lebanese Muhammara

Prep time: 15 minutes / Cook time: 15 minutes
Serves 6

Ingredients:
- 2 large red bell peppers • 5ml (1 teaspoon) kosher salt
- 180ml (¼ cup plus 2 tablespoons) extra-virgin olive oil
- 120g (1 cup) walnut halves
- 1 tablespoon agave nectar or honey
- 5ml (1 teaspoon) fresh lemon juice
- 5ml (1 teaspoon) ground cumin
- 5ml (1 teaspoon) red pepper flakes
- Raw vegetables (such as cucumber, carrots, zucchini slices, or cauliflower) or toasted pita chips, for serving

Instructions:
1. Begin by drizzling the red bell peppers with 2 tablespoons of olive oil and placing them in the air fryer basket. Set the air fryer to 400ºF (204ºC) and cook for 10 minutes.
2. After 10 minutes, add the walnut halves to the basket, arranging them around the peppers. Set the air fryer to 400ºF (204ºC) again and cook for 5 more minutes.
3. Remove the peppers from the air fryer, seal them in a resealable plastic bag, and let them rest for 5 to 10 minutes. Transfer the walnuts to a plate and allow them to cool.
4. In a food processor, combine the softened peppers, cooled walnuts, agave nectar (or honey), lemon juice, ground cumin, kosher salt, and ½ teaspoon of red pepper flakes. Purée until smooth.
5. Transfer the dip to a serving bowl and create an indentation in the middle. Pour the remaining ¼ cup of olive oil into the indentation. Garnish the dip with the remaining ½ teaspoon of red pepper flakes.
6. Serve the muhammara with raw vegetables or toasted pita chips.

Nutritional Information (Per Serving): Calories: 219 / Fat: 20g / Protein: 3g / Carbs: 9g / Fiber: 2g / Sodium: 391mg

Tex-Mex Style Tortilla Chips

Prep time: 5 minutes / Cook time: 5 minutes
Serves 4

Ingredients:
• Olive oil
• 2.5g (1/2 teaspoon) salt
• 2.5g (1/2 teaspoon) ground cumin
• 2.5g (1/2 teaspoon) chili powder
• 2.5g (1/2 teaspoon) paprika
• Pinch of cayenne pepper
• 8 (6-inch) corn tortillas, each cut into 6 wedges

Instructions:
1. Lightly spray the air fryer basket with olive oil.
2. In a small bowl, mix together the salt, cumin, chili powder, paprika, and cayenne pepper.
3. Arrange the tortilla wedges in a single layer in the air fryer basket. Lightly spray the tortillas with oil and sprinkle some of the seasoning mixture over them. You may need to cook the tortillas in batches.
4. Air fry at 375ºF (191ºC) for 2 to 3 minutes. Shake the basket and continue cooking until the chips are golden brown and crispy, for an additional 2 to 3 minutes. Keep an eye on them to prevent burning.
5. Once cooked, transfer the chips to a serving plate and serve immediately.

*Nutritional Information (Per Serving):*Calories: 118 / Fat: 1g / Protein: 3g / Carbs. 25g / Fiber: 3g / Sodium: 307mg

Cinnamon-Apple Chips

Prep time: 10 minutes / Cook time: 32 minutes
Serves 4

Ingredients:
• Oil, for spraying
• 2 Red Delicious or Honeycrisp apples
• 1/4 teaspoon ground cinnamon, divided

Instructions:
1. Lightly spray the air fryer basket with oil and line it with parchment paper.
2. Trim the uneven ends off the apples, then thinly slice them using a mandoline on the thinnest setting or a sharp knife. Discard the cores.
3. Arrange half of the apple slices in a single layer in the prepared basket and sprinkle them with half of the cinnamon.
4. Place a metal air fryer trivet on top of the apples to prevent them from moving around during cooking.
5. Air fry at 300ºF (149ºC) for 16 minutes, flipping the slices every 5 minutes to ensure even cooking. Repeat with the remaining apple slices and cinnamon.
6. Allow the chips to cool to room temperature before serving. They will become firmer as they cool.

*Nutritional Information (Per Serving):*Calories: 63 / Fat: 0g / Protein: 0g / Carbs: 15g / Fiber: 3g / Sodium: 1mg

Shrimp Pirogues

Prep time: 15 minutes / Cook time: 4 to 5 minutes
Serves 8

Ingredients:
- 12 ounces (340 g) small, peeled, and deveined raw shrimp
- 3 ounces (85 g) cream cheese, room temperature
- 2 tablespoons plain yogurt • 1 teaspoon lemon juice
- 1 teaspoon dried dill weed, crushed
- Salt, to taste • 4 small hothouse cucumbers, each approximately 6 inches long

Instructions:
1. Pour 4 tablespoons of water into the bottom of the air fryer drawer.
2. Arrange the shrimp in a single layer in the air fryer basket and air fry at 390ºF (199ºC) for 4 to 5 minutes until just cooked. Be attentive as shrimp cooks quickly.
3. Chop the cooked shrimp into small pieces, no larger than ½ inch, and refrigerate.
4. Mash and whip the cream cheese until smooth using a fork.
5. Stir in the yogurt until smooth, then add lemon juice, crushed dill weed, and chopped shrimp, mixing well.
6. Taste and adjust seasoning with salt if necessary, adding ¼ to ½ teaspoon as desired.
7. Refrigerate the shrimp mixture until ready to serve.
8. Before serving, wash and dry the cucumbers, then split them lengthwise and scoop out the seeds. Drain them upside down on paper towels for 10 minutes.
9. Pat the cucumber centers dry before filling. Spoon the shrimp mixture into the cucumbers and cut them in half crosswise. Serve immediately.

Nutritional Information (Per Serving): Calories: 85 / Fat: 4g / Protein: 10g / Carbs: 2g / Fiber: 1g / Sodium: 93mg

Garlic-Roasted Mushrooms

Prep time: 3 minutes / Cook time: 22 to 27 minutes
Serves 4

Ingredients:
- 16 garlic cloves, peeled
- 2 teaspoons olive oil, divided
- 16 button mushrooms
- ½ teaspoon dried marjoram
- ⅛ teaspoon freshly ground black pepper
- 1 tablespoon white wine or low-sodium vegetable broth

Instructions:
1. Preheat the air fryer to 350ºF (177ºC).
2. In a baking pan, toss the garlic cloves with 1 teaspoon of olive oil. Roast in the air fryer for 12 minutes.
3. Add the mushrooms, marjoram, and black pepper to the pan. Drizzle with the remaining teaspoon of olive oil and the white wine or vegetable broth. Toss to coat.
4. Return the pan to the air fryer and roast for an additional 10 to 15 minutes, or until the mushrooms and garlic cloves are tender.
5. Serve the roasted mushrooms and garlic cloves immediately.

Nutritional Information (Per Serving): Calories: 57 / Fat: 3g / Protein: 3g / Carbs: 7g / Fiber: 1g / Sodium: 6mg

Curried Yogurt Greens Chips

Prep time: 10 minutes / Cook time: 5 to 6 minutes
Serves 4

Ingredients:
- 240g (1 cup) low-fat Greek yogurt
- 15ml (1 tablespoon) freshly squeezed lemon juice
- 8g (1 tablespoon) curry powder
- ½ bunch curly kale, stemmed, ribs removed and discarded, leaves cut into 2- to 3-inch pieces
- ½ bunch chard, stemmed, ribs removed and discarded, leaves cut into 2- to 3-inch pieces
- 7.5ml (1½ teaspoons) olive oil

Instructions:
1. In a small bowl, mix together the low-fat Greek yogurt, lemon juice, and curry powder. Set aside.
2. In a large bowl, combine the curly kale and chard with olive oil, ensuring the leaves are evenly coated. Massage the oil into the leaves to tenderize them.
3. Air fry the greens in batches at 390ºF (199ºC) for 5 to 6 minutes until crisp, shaking the basket once during cooking to ensure even crisping.
4. Serve the crispy greens chips with the prepared curried yogurt sauce.

Nutritional Information (Per Serving): Calories: 98 / Fat: 4g / Protein: 7g / Carbs: 13g / Fiber: 4g / Sodium: 186mg

Savory Black Bean Corn Dip

Prep time: 10 minutes / Cook time: 10 minutes
Serves 4

Ingredients:
- 213g (1/2 cup) canned black beans, drained and rinsed
- 213g (1/2 cup) canned corn, drained and rinsed
- 60ml (1/4 cup) chunky salsa
- 57g (2 ounces) reduced-fat cream cheese, softened
- 28g (1/4 cup) shredded reduced-fat Cheddar cheese
- 1/2 teaspoon ground cumin
- 1/2 teaspoon paprika
- Salt and freshly ground black pepper, to taste

Instructions:
1. Preheat the air fryer to 325ºF (163ºC).
2. In a medium bowl, combine the drained and rinsed black beans, corn, chunky salsa, softened reduced-fat cream cheese, shredded reduced-fat Cheddar cheese, ground cumin, and paprika. Season with salt and pepper, then stir until well mixed.
3. Spoon the mixture into a baking dish.
4. Place the baking dish in the air fryer basket and bake until heated through, approximately 10 minutes.
5. Serve the hot dip immediately

Nutritional Information (Per Serving): Calories: 119 / Fat: 2g / Protein: 8g / Carbs: 19g / Fiber: 6g / Sodium: 469mg

Mediterranean Herb Okra Chips

Prep time: 10 minutes / Cook time: 20 minutes
Serves 4

Ingredients:
- 500g (about 4 cups) okra, trimmed, washed, and sliced into halves
- 60g (1/2 cup) cornmeal
- 15g (1 tablespoon) flaxseed meal
- 15g (1 tablespoon) Mediterranean herb mix
- 30ml (2 tablespoons) extra-virgin olive oil
- Sea salt and ground black pepper, to taste

Instructions:
1. Wash the okra thoroughly and trim the ends. Slice them lengthwise into halves.
2. In a large mixing bowl, combine the okra halves with the extra-virgin olive oil, cornmeal, flaxseed meal, Mediterranean herb mix, sea salt, and ground black pepper. Toss until the okra is evenly coated with the mixture.
3. Preheat your Air Fryer to 180 degrees C (350 degrees F). Place the coated okra in the Air Fryer basket in a single layer, ensuring they are not overcrowded. Cook for about 20 minutes, shaking the basket occasionally to promote even cooking and crispiness.
4. Once the okra is golden brown and crispy, remove it from the Air Fryer. Serve immediately as a delicious snack or side dish.

Nutritional Information (Per Serving): Calories: 178 / Fat: 8.6g / Carbs: 23.3g / Fiber: 5.5g / Protein: 4.2g

Roasted Beet Salad with Goat Cheese

Prep time: 10 minutes / Cook time: 40 minutes
Serves 4

Ingredients:
- 4 cups (about 500g) mixed beets (golden, red, purple), peeled and sliced
- 2 tbsp extra-virgin olive oil
- 1 tbsp fresh lemon juice
- 1 tbsp red wine vinegar
- 1 tbsp Dijon mustard
- 2 garlic cloves, minced
- 1/2 tsp ground cumin
- Sea salt and ground black pepper, to taste
- 1/2 small bunch parsley, roughly chopped
- 4.2 oz (120g) goat cheese, crumbled

Instructions:
1. Preheat your air fryer to 200°C (390°F).
2. Place the sliced beets in a single layer in the lightly greased air fryer basket.
3. Cook the beets in the air fryer for 40 minutes, shaking the basket halfway through the cooking time.
4. Let the beets cool at room temperature, then transfer them to a mixing bowl.
5. In a small bowl, whisk together the olive oil, lemon juice, red wine vinegar, Dijon mustard, minced garlic, ground cumin, sea salt, and black pepper.
6. Pour the dressing over the cooled beets and toss until well coated.
7. Chill the salad in the fridge until ready to serve.
8. Just before serving, sprinkle the crumbled goat cheese and chopped parsley over the salad.
9. Enjoy!

Nutritional Information (Per Serving): / Calories: 264 / Fat: 17.6g / Carbs: 15.3g / Fiber: 5.5g / Protein: 12g

Harissa Courgette and Corn Latkes

Prep time: 10 minutes / Cook time: 20 minutes
Serves 4

Ingredients:

- 1 cup (about 100g) grated and squeezed courgette (zucchini)
- 1 cup (about 150g) canned sweetcorn, drained
- 2 spring onions, finely chopped
- 1 cup (about 100g) semolina flour
- 1 large egg, beaten
- 2 tbsp Harissa sauce
- 1 tbsp dried rosemary
- 1 tsp fried sage
- 1 tbsp olive oil
- Sea salt and ground black pepper, to taste

Instructions:

1. In a mixing bowl, combine the grated courgette, sweetcorn, spring onions, semolina flour, beaten egg, Harissa sauce, dried rosemary, fried sage, olive oil, sea salt, and black pepper. Mix until all ingredients are well incorporated.
2. Spoon burger-sized mounds of the mixture onto a parchment-lined air fryer basket.
3. Air fry the latkes at 190°C (375°F) for 20 minutes or until cooked through and crispy.
4. Serve hot and enjoy!

Nutritional Information (Per Serving): / Calories: 284 / Fat: 12.6g / Carbs: 29.8g / Fiber: 2.5g / Protein: 13.2g

Grilled Prawn Kabobs

Prep time: 10 minutes + marinating time / Cook time: 12 minutes
Serves 4

Ingredients:

- 500g extra-large prawns, peeled and deveined (about 5 cups)
- 1 garlic clove, crushed
- 1 tsp ground coriander
- 1 tbsp dried rosemary
- 1 tbsp dried basil
- Juice of 1 medium lemon
- 2 tbsp white cooking wine
- 1 tbsp Dijon mustard
- 2 tsp extra-virgin olive oil

Instructions:

1. In a ceramic or glass bowl, combine the prawns with the crushed garlic, ground coriander, dried rosemary, dried basil, lemon juice, white cooking wine, Dijon mustard, and extra-virgin olive oil. Toss until the prawns are evenly coated. Cover and refrigerate for about 30 minutes to marinate.
2. Thread the marinated prawns onto bamboo skewers that have been soaked in water.
3. Preheat your air fryer to 200°C (390°F).
4. Cook the prawn kabobs in the air fryer for 12 minutes, shaking the basket halfway through the cooking time to ensure even cooking.
5. Serve the warm kabobs with your favorite sauce for dipping, if desired.
6. Enjoy!

Nutritional Information (Per Serving): / Calories: 142 / Fat: 3.1g / Carbs: 2.8g / Fiber: 0.6g / Protein: 25.9g

Chapter 6: Vegetable and Side Dish Recipes

Roasted Broccoli Salad

Prep time: 5 minutes / Cook time: 7 minutes Serves 4

Ingredients:
- 500g (about 4 cups) fresh broccoli florets, chopped
- 15ml (1 tablespoon) olive oil
- ¼ teaspoon salt
- ⅛ teaspoon ground black pepper
- 60ml (¼ cup) lemon juice, divided
- 30g (¼ cup) shredded Parmesan cheese
- 30g (¼ cup) sliced roasted almonds

Instructions:
1. In a large bowl, combine the chopped broccoli and olive oil. Sprinkle with salt and pepper, then drizzle with 2 tablespoons of lemon juice.
2. Transfer the broccoli to the air fryer basket. Set the temperature to 350ºF (177ºC) and cook for 7 minutes, shaking the basket halfway through cooking. The broccoli should be golden on the edges when done.
3. Place the cooked broccoli into a large serving bowl and drizzle with the remaining lemon juice. Sprinkle with Parmesan cheese and sliced almonds. Serve warm.

Nutritional Information (Per Serving): Calories: 76 / Fat: 5g / Protein: 3g / Carbs: 5g / Fiber: 1g / Sodium: 273mg

Spinach and Sweet Pepper Poppers

Prep time: 10 minutes / Cook time: 8 minutes / Makes 16 poppers

Ingredients:
- 113g (4 ounces) cream cheese, softened
- 1 cup chopped fresh spinach leaves
- 2.5ml (1/2 teaspoon) garlic powder
- 8 mini sweet bell peppers, tops removed, seeded, and halved lengthwise

Instructions:
1. In a medium bowl, combine softened cream cheese, chopped spinach, and garlic powder until well mixed.
2. Spoon 1 tablespoon of the cream cheese mixture into each halved sweet pepper, pressing down gently to smooth the top.
3. Arrange the stuffed peppers in the ungreased air fryer basket.
4. Adjust the air fryer temperature to 400ºF (204ºC) and cook for 8 minutes until the cheese is browned on top and the peppers are tender-crisp.
5. Serve the poppers warm.

Nutritional Information (Per Serving): Calories: 31 / Fat: 2g / Protein: 1g / Carbs: 3g / Fiber: 0g / Sodium: 34mg

Roasted Cauliflower with Tahini Sauce

Prep time: 10 minutes / Cook time: 20 minutes
Serves 4

Ingredients:

Cauliflower:
- 600g (about 5 cups) cauliflower florets (approximately 1 large head)
- 6 garlic cloves, smashed and cut into thirds
- 45ml (3 tablespoons) vegetable oil
- 2.5ml (1/2 teaspoon) ground cumin
- 2.5ml (1/2 teaspoon) ground coriander
- 2.5ml (1/2 teaspoon) kosher salt

Sauce:
- 30g (2 tablespoons) tahini (sesame paste)
- 30ml (2 tablespoons) hot water
- 15ml (1 tablespoon) fresh lemon juice
- 5g (1 teaspoon) minced garlic
- 2.5ml (1/2 teaspoon) kosher salt

Instructions:

1. In a large bowl, combine the cauliflower florets and smashed garlic. Drizzle with vegetable oil and sprinkle with ground cumin, ground coriander, and kosher salt. Toss until the cauliflower is evenly coated.
2. Place the seasoned cauliflower in the air fryer basket. Set the air fryer to 400°F (204°C) for 20 minutes, turning the cauliflower halfway through the cooking time.
3. While the cauliflower is cooking, prepare the sauce. In a small bowl, whisk together tahini, hot water, lemon juice, minced garlic, and kosher salt until you have a thick, creamy, smooth mixture.
4. Once the cauliflower is done, transfer it to a large serving bowl. Pour the tahini sauce over the cauliflower and toss gently to coat.
5. Serve the roasted cauliflower with tahini sauce immediately.

Nutritional Information (Per Serving): Calories: 176 / Fat: 15g / Protein: 4g / Carbs: 10g / Fiber: 4g / Sodium: 632mg

Roasted Beets with Chermoula

Prep time: 15 minutes / Cook time: 25 minutes
Serves 4

Ingredients:

Chermoula:
- 1 cup packed fresh cilantro leaves
- ½ cup packed fresh parsley leaves
- 6 cloves garlic, peeled
- 2 teaspoons smoked paprika
- 2 teaspoons ground cumin
- 1 teaspoon ground coriander
- ½ to 1 teaspoon cayenne pepper
- Pinch of crushed saffron (optional)
- 120ml (½ cup) extra-virgin olive oil
- Kosher salt, to taste

Beets:
- 500g (about 3 medium) beets, trimmed, peeled, and cut into 1-inch chunks
- 2 tablespoons chopped fresh cilantro
- 2 tablespoons chopped fresh parsley

Instructions:

1. To prepare the chermoula, in a food processor, combine the cilantro, parsley, garlic, paprika, cumin, coriander, and cayenne. Pulse until coarsely chopped. Add the saffron, if using, and process until combined. With the food processor running, slowly add the olive oil in a steady stream; process until the sauce is uniform. Season to taste with salt.
2. For the beets, in a large bowl, drizzle the beet chunks with ½ cup of the chermoula, or enough to coat them. Arrange the beets in the air fryer basket. Set the air fryer to 375°F (191°C) for 25 minutes, or until the beets are tender.
3. Transfer the roasted beets to a serving platter. Sprinkle with chopped cilantro and parsley and serve.

Nutritional Information (Per Serving): Calories: 61 / Fat: 2g / Protein: 2g / Carbs: 9g / Fiber: 3g / Sodium: 59mg

Spiced Sweet Potato Cubes

Prep time: 10 minutes / Cook time: 12 minutes
Serves 4

Ingredients:
- 2 large sweet potatoes, peeled and cut into ¾-inch cubes (about 3 cups)
- 15ml (1 tablespoon) olive oil
- ½ teaspoon ground cinnamon
- ¼ teaspoon ground cumin
- ¼ teaspoon paprika
- 1 teaspoon chile powder
- ⅛ teaspoon turmeric
- ½ teaspoon salt (optional)
- Freshly ground black pepper, to taste

Instructions:
1. In a large bowl, combine ground cinnamon, ground cumin, paprika, chile powder, turmeric, salt (if using), and freshly ground black pepper.
2. Add the sweet potato cubes to the bowl and toss until they are evenly coated with the spice mixture.
3. Drizzle olive oil over the seasoned sweet potatoes and toss again until they are well coated.
4. Transfer the seasoned sweet potatoes to a baking pan or an ovenproof dish that fits inside the air fryer basket.
5. Air fry at 390ºF (199ºC) for 6 minutes, then pause to stir well.
6. Continue air frying for an additional 6 minutes or until the sweet potatoes are tender and lightly browned.
7. Serve hot.

Nutritional Information (Per Serving): Calories: 141 / Fat: 4g / Protein: 2g / Carbs: 26g / Fiber: 4g / Sodium: 327mg

Zucchini Fritters

Prep time: 10 minutes / Cook time: 10 minutes
Serves 4

Ingredients:
- 454g (about 2 cups) grated zucchini
- 1 teaspoon salt
- 60g (1/4 cup) almond flour
- 25g (1/4 cup) grated Parmesan cheese
- 1 large egg
- 1/4 teaspoon dried thyme
- 1/4 teaspoon ground turmeric
- 1/4 teaspoon freshly ground black pepper
- 15ml (1 tablespoon) olive oil
- 1/2 lemon, sliced into wedges

Instructions:
1. Preheat the air fryer to 400ºF (204ºC). Cut a piece of parchment paper to fit slightly smaller than the bottom of the air fryer.
2. Place the grated zucchini in a large colander and sprinkle with salt. Let it sit for 5 to 10 minutes. Squeeze out as much liquid as possible from the zucchini and transfer it to a large mixing bowl. Add almond flour, Parmesan cheese, egg, thyme, turmeric, and black pepper. Gently stir until well combined.
3. Shape the mixture into 8 patties and place them on the parchment paper. Lightly brush the patties with olive oil. Air fry for 10 minutes, turning the patties halfway through the cooking time until they are golden brown. Serve warm with lemon wedges.

Nutritional Information (Per Serving): Calories: 78 / Fat: 6g / Protein: 4g / Carbs: 2g / Fiber: 0g / Sodium: 712mg

Homemade Roasted Salsa

Prep time: 15 minutes / Cook time: 30 minutes / Makes 2 cups

Ingredients:
- 2 large San Marzano tomatoes, cored and chopped into large chunks
- 1/2 medium white onion, peeled and diced into large pieces
- 1/2 medium jalapeño, seeded and diced into large pieces
- 2 cloves garlic, peeled and minced
- 1/2 teaspoon salt
- 1 tablespoon coconut oil
- 60ml (1/4 cup) fresh lime juice

Instructions:
1. In an ungreased round nonstick baking dish, place the tomatoes, onion, jalapeño, and garlic. Sprinkle with salt and drizzle with coconut oil.
2. Put the baking dish into the air fryer basket. Set the temperature to 300ºF (149ºC) and roast for 30 minutes until the vegetables are tender and have browned edges.
3. Transfer the roasted vegetables to a food processor or blender. Add lime juice and process on low speed for about 30 seconds until the salsa is slightly chunky.
4. Pour the salsa into a sealable container and refrigerate for at least 1 hour before serving. Serve chilled.

Nutritional Information (Per Serving):Calories: 115 / Fat: 7g / Protein: 2g / Carbs: 13g / Fiber: 3g / Sodium: 593mg

Honey Sesame Glazed Carrots and Sugar Snap Peas

Prep time: 10 minutes / Cook time: 16 minutes Serves 4

Ingredients:
- 454g (1 pound) carrots, peeled and sliced on the bias (about 2 cups)
- 1 teaspoon olive oil
- Salt and freshly ground black pepper, to taste
- 80ml (1/3 cup) honey
- 15ml (1 tablespoon) sesame oil
- 15ml (1 tablespoon) soy sauce
- 1/2 teaspoon minced fresh ginger
- 113g (4 ounces) sugar snap peas (about 1 cup)
- 1 1/2 teaspoons sesame seeds

Instructions:
1. Preheat the air fryer to 360ºF (182ºC).
2. In a bowl, toss the carrots with olive oil, salt, and pepper. Air fry for 10 minutes, shaking the basket occasionally.
3. In a large bowl, combine honey, sesame oil, soy sauce, and minced ginger. Add the sugar snap peas and air-fried carrots to the mixture. Toss to coat.
4. Return everything to the air fryer basket and increase the temperature to 400ºF (204ºC). Air fry for an additional 6 minutes, shaking the basket halfway through.
5. Transfer the glazed carrots and sugar snap peas to a serving bowl. Pour the sauce from the bottom of the cooker over the vegetables and sprinkle sesame seeds on top. Serve immediately.

Nutritional Information (Per Serving):Calories: 202 / Fat: 6g / Protein: 2g / Carbs: 37g / Fiber: 4g / Sodium: 141mg

Herbed Shiitake Mushrooms

Prep time: 10 minutes / Cook time: 5 minutes
Serves 4

Ingredients:
- 227g (8 ounces) shiitake mushrooms, stems removed and caps roughly chopped
- 15ml (1 tablespoon) olive oil
- 2.5ml (1/2 teaspoon) salt
- Freshly ground black pepper, to taste
- 1 teaspoon chopped fresh thyme leaves
- 1 teaspoon chopped fresh oregano
- 15ml (1 tablespoon) chopped fresh parsley

Instructions:
1. Preheat the air fryer to 400ºF (204ºC).
2. In a bowl, toss the shiitake mushrooms with olive oil, salt, pepper, thyme, and oregano until evenly coated.
3. Air fry for 5 minutes, shaking the basket occasionally for even cooking. The mushrooms should have a somewhat chewy texture with a meaty consistency. If you prefer them softer, you can add a couple more minutes to the cooking time.
4. Once cooked, add the chopped parsley to the mushrooms and toss to combine.
5. Adjust seasoning with salt and pepper to taste if needed, then serve immediately.

*Nutritional Information (Per Serving):*Calories: 50 / Fat: 4g / Protein: 1g / Carbs: 4g / Fiber: 2g / Sodium: 296mg

Fiery Chili-Roasted Broccoli

Prep time: 5 minutes / Cook time: 10 minutes
Serves 2

Ingredients:
- 340g (12 ounces) broccoli florets
- 30ml (2 tablespoons) Asian hot chili oil
- 5g (1 teaspoon) ground Sichuan peppercorns (or black pepper)
- 2 cloves garlic, finely chopped
- 1 (2-inch) piece fresh ginger, peeled and finely chopped
- Kosher salt and freshly ground black pepper, to taste

Instructions:
1. In a bowl, combine broccoli florets, chili oil, ground Sichuan peppercorns, chopped garlic, chopped ginger, and season with salt and black pepper to taste.
2. Transfer the seasoned broccoli to the air fryer and roast at 375ºF (191ºC) for about 10 minutes, shaking the basket halfway through, until lightly charred and tender.
3. Once done, remove the chili-roasted broccoli from the air fryer and serve warm.

*Nutritional Information (Per Serving):*Calories: 141 / Fat: 9g / Protein: 5g / Carbs: 13g / Fiber: 5g / Sodium: 57mg

Salad Recipes

Green Bean Tomato Salad

Prep time: 10 minutes / Cook time: 11 minutes
Serves 4

Ingredients:
- 10.5 oz (300g) green beans, cleaned and trimmed
- 3.5 oz (100g) cherry tomatoes
- 1 bell pepper, deseeded and halved
- 1 small red onion, sliced
- 3.5 oz (100g) Pecorino cheese, grated
- 2 tbsp extra-virgin olive oil
- 1 tsp Aleppo pepper
- 1 tsp dried oregano
- 1 tsp dried rosemary
- Flaky sea salt and ground black pepper, to taste

Instructions:
1. Preheat your Air Fryer to 200 degrees C.
2. In a large bowl, toss the green beans and cherry tomatoes with 1 tablespoon of olive oil, Aleppo pepper, dried oregano, dried rosemary, flaky sea salt, and ground black pepper. Ensure they are well coated on all sides.
3. Place the seasoned green beans and cherry tomatoes in the preheated Air Fryer and cook for 11 minutes.
4. Once cooked, remove the green beans and cherry tomatoes from the Air Fryer and transfer them to a serving dish.
5. Add the bell pepper, sliced red onion, and grated Pecorino cheese to the dish with the green beans and cherry tomatoes. Toss gently to combine.
6. Serve the green bean tomato salad and enjoy!

Nutritional Information (Per Serving): Calories: 222 / Fat: 16g / Carbs: 11.6g / Fiber: 3.3g / Protein: 8.4g

Warm Sweet Potato Salad

Prep time: 10 minutes / Cook time: 20 minutes
Serves 4

Ingredients:
- 14.1 oz (400g) sweet potatoes, peeled and diced
- 2 tbsp extra-virgin olive oil
- 4 spring onions, sliced
- 1 tsp dried dill
- 2 tbsp cider vinegar
- 2 tbsp honey
- Sea salt and ground black pepper, to taste

Instructions:
1. Preheat your Air Fryer to 190 degrees C.
2. In a large bowl, toss the diced sweet potatoes with 1 tablespoon of olive oil, sea salt, and ground black pepper until they are well coated on all sides.
3. Place the seasoned sweet potatoes in the preheated Air Fryer and cook for 20 minutes.
4. Once cooked, remove the sweet potatoes from the Air Fryer and let them cool slightly.
5. Transfer the cooked sweet potatoes to a salad bowl.
6. Add the sliced spring onions, dried dill, cider vinegar, honey, and the remaining 1 tablespoon of olive oil to the salad bowl.
7. Gently stir the ingredients to combine.
8. Serve the warm sweet potato salad and enjoy!

Nutritional Information (Per Serving): Calories: 183 / Fat: 7.2g / Carbs: 28.3g / Fiber: 3g / Protein: 2.6g

Restaurant-Style Greek Salad

**Prep time: 10 minutes / Cook time: 5 minutes
Serves 2**

Ingredients:
- 1/2 small corn Mediterranean bread, cut into bite-sized cubes
- 60g Kalamata olives, stoned and sliced
- 1 ripe tomato, diced
- 1 medium red onion, thinly sliced
- 1 medium Greek cucumber, sliced
- 40g feta cheese, crumbled
- 2 tbsp capers
- 2 tbsp extra-virgin olive oil
- 1 tsp garlic granules
- 1 tsp dried oregano
- Flaky sea salt and ground black pepper, to taste

Instructions:
1. Preheat your Air Fryer to 200 degrees C.
2. In a bowl, toss the bite-sized bread cubes with 1 tablespoon of olive oil, garlic granules, dried oregano, flaky sea salt, and ground black pepper until they are well coated on all sides.
3. Place the seasoned bread cubes in the preheated Air Fryer and toast for 5 minutes. Remember to shake the basket halfway through the cooking time.
4. Once toasted, transfer the croutons to a paper towel-lined plate and set aside.
5. In a salad bowl, combine the diced tomato, thinly sliced red onion, sliced Greek cucumber, sliced Kalamata olives, crumbled feta cheese, and capers.
6. Top the salad with the prepared croutons.
7. Toss all the ingredients together.
8. Serve the restaurant-style Greek salad and enjoy!

Nutritional Information (Per Serving):Calories: 515 / Fat: 26.3g / Carbs: 58.4g / Fiber: 5.5g / Protein: 13.7g

Basic Okra Salad

**Prep time: 10 minutes / Cook time: 18 minutes
Serves 4**

Ingredients:
- 17.6 oz (500g) okra, cleaned and trimmed
- 1 large head of romaine lettuce, torn into pieces
- 1 small cucumber, sliced
- 1 medium tomato, sliced
- 80g cornmeal
- 2 tbsp extra-virgin olive oil
- 1/2 tsp ground coriander
- 1 tsp Aleppo pepper
- Sea salt and ground black pepper, to taste

Instructions:
1. Preheat your Air Fryer to 180 degrees C.
2. Cut the okra into halves lengthwise.
3. In a bowl, toss the okra halves with 1 tablespoon of olive oil, cornmeal, ground coriander, Aleppo pepper, sea salt, and ground black pepper until they are well coated on all sides.
4. Place the seasoned okra in the preheated Air Fryer and cook for 18 minutes, shaking the basket once or twice during cooking to ensure even cooking.
5. Once cooked, remove the okra from the Air Fryer and let it cool slightly.
6. In a large salad bowl, combine the cooked okra with the torn romaine lettuce, sliced cucumber, and sliced tomato.
7. Toss all the ingredients together until well combined.
8. Serve the basic okra salad and enjoy!

Nutritional Information (Per Serving):Calories: 216 / Fat: 8.2g / Carbs: 33.5g / Fiber: 7.7g / Protein: 6.7g

Cheese Green Bean Salad

Prep time: 10 minutes / Cook time: 25 minutes
Serves 4

Ingredients:
- 14.1 oz (400g) green beans, cleaned and trimmed
- 1 bell pepper, deseeded and halved
- 1 medium tomato, sliced
- 1 small red onion, sliced
- 3.5 oz (100g) goat's milk cheese, crumbled (hard type)
- 2 tbsp extra-virgin olive oil
- 1 tsp red pepper flakes, crushed
- Flaky sea salt and ground black pepper, to taste

Instructions:
1. Preheat your Air Fryer to 200 degrees C.
2. In a bowl, toss the cleaned and trimmed green beans with 1 tablespoon of olive oil, crushed red pepper flakes, flaky sea salt, and ground black pepper until they are well coated on all sides.
3. Place the seasoned green beans in the preheated Air Fryer and cook for 25 minutes, shaking the basket halfway through cooking.
4. Once cooked, remove the green beans from the Air Fryer and let them cool slightly.
5. In a salad bowl, combine the cooked green beans with the halved bell pepper, sliced tomato, and sliced red onion.
6. Toss all the ingredients together until well combined.
7. Top the salad with crumbled goat's milk cheese.
8. Serve the cheese green bean salad and enjoy!

*Nutritional Information (Per Serving):*Calories: 232 / Fat: 16.1g / Carbs: 13.3g / Fiber: 4.3g / Protein: 10.5g

Arugula, Chickpea, and Feta Salad

Prep time: 10 minutes / Cook time: 14 minutes
Serves 4

Ingredients:
- 7 oz (200g) chickpeas, canned or cooked, drained and rinsed
- 7 oz (200g) arugula
- 1 small cucumber, sliced
- 1 medium tomato, sliced
- 4.2 oz (120g) feta cheese, crumbled
- 2 tbsp extra-virgin olive oil
- 1 tsp crushed red pepper flakes
- 1/2 tsp ground coriander
- Sea salt and ground black pepper, to taste

Instructions:
1. Preheat your Air Fryer to 180 degrees C.
2. In a bowl, toss the drained and rinsed chickpeas with 1 tablespoon of olive oil, crushed red pepper flakes, ground coriander, sea salt, and ground black pepper until they are well coated on all sides.
3. Place the seasoned chickpeas in the preheated Air Fryer and roast for 14 minutes, shaking the basket once or twice during cooking to ensure even cooking.
4. Once the chickpeas are roasted, remove them from the Air Fryer and let them cool slightly.
5. In a salad bowl, combine the roasted chickpeas with the arugula, sliced cucumber, sliced tomato, and crumbled feta cheese.
6. Toss all the ingredients together until well combined.
7. Serve the arugula, chickpea, and feta salad and enjoy!

*Nutritional Information (Per Serving):*Calories: 241 / Fat: 14.8g / Carbs: 18.5g / Fiber: 4.7g / Protein: 10.7g

Chapter 7: Vegetarian Main Course Recipes

Mediterranean Pan Pizza

Prep time: 5 minutes / Cook time: 8 minutes
Serves 2

Ingredients:
- 1 cup shredded Mozzarella cheese (100g)
- ¼ medium red bell pepper, chopped (about 30g)
- ½ cup chopped fresh spinach leaves (about 30g)
- 2 tablespoons chopped black olives (about 15g)
- 2 tablespoons crumbled feta cheese (about 15g)

Instructions:
1. Spread the shredded Mozzarella cheese evenly in an ungreased round nonstick baking dish. Layer the chopped red bell pepper, fresh spinach leaves, black olives, and crumbled feta cheese on top of the Mozzarella.
2. Place the baking dish into the air fryer basket. Set the temperature to 350°F (177°C) and bake for 8 minutes. Check halfway through to prevent burning. The top of the pizza should turn golden brown, and the cheese should be melted when done.
3. Once cooked, remove the dish from the air fryer and allow it to cool for 5 minutes before slicing and serving.

Nutritional Information (Per Serving): Calories: 108 / Fat: 1g / Protein: 20g / Carbs: 5g / Fiber: 3g / Sodium: 521mg

Homemade Vegetable Burgers

Prep time: 10 minutes / Cook time: 12 minutes
Serves 4

Ingredients:
- 8 ounces (227 g) cremini mushrooms
- 2 large egg yolks
- ½ medium zucchini, chopped (about 120g)
- ¼ cup yellow onion, chopped (about 40g)
- 1 clove garlic, finely minced
- ½ teaspoon salt
- ¼ teaspoon ground black pepper

Instructions:
1. Combine all ingredients in a food processor and pulse twenty times until finely chopped and well combined.
2. Divide the mixture into four equal portions and shape each into a burger patty. Place the patties in the ungreased air fryer basket. Set the temperature to 375°F (191°C) and air fry for 12 minutes, flipping the burgers halfway through cooking. They should be browned and firm.
3. Once cooked, transfer the burgers to a large plate and let them cool for 5 minutes before serving.

Nutritional Information (Per Serving): Calories: 50 / Fat: 3g / Protein: 3g / Carbs: 4g / Fiber: 1g / Sodium: 299mg

Homemade Pesto Spinach Flatbread

Prep time: 10 minutes / Cook time: 8 minutes
Serves 4

Ingredients:
- 120g (1 cup) blanched finely ground almond flour
- 57g (2 ounces) cream cheese
- 226g (2 cups) shredded Mozzarella cheese
- 30g (1 cup) chopped fresh spinach leaves
- 30g (2 tablespoons) basil pesto

Instructions:
1. In a large microwave-safe bowl, combine the almond flour, cream cheese, and shredded Mozzarella. Microwave on high for 45 seconds, then stir the mixture.
2. Add the chopped spinach to the bowl and microwave for an additional 15 seconds. Stir until a soft dough ball forms.
3. Cut two pieces of parchment paper to fit the air fryer basket. Divide the dough into two portions and press each portion into a 6-inch round on separate pieces of parchment paper.
4. Spread 1 tablespoon of basil pesto over each flatbread and transfer the rounds, parchment paper and all, into the ungreased air fryer basket. Set the temperature to 350ºF (177ºC) and air fry for 8 minutes, flipping the flatbreads halfway through cooking. They should turn golden brown.
5. Allow the flatbreads to cool for 5 minutes before slicing and serving.

*Nutritional Information (Per Serving):*Calories: 387 / Fat: 28g / Protein: 28g / Carbs: 10g / Fiber: 5g / Sodium: 556mg

Crustless Spinach Cheese Pie

Prep time: 10 minutes / Cook time: 20 minutes
Serves 4

Ingredients:
- 6 large eggs
- 60ml (1/4 cup) heavy whipping cream
- 110g (1 cup) frozen chopped spinach, drained
- 120g (1 cup) shredded sharp Cheddar cheese
- 60g (1/4 cup) diced yellow onion

Instructions:
1. In a medium bowl, whisk together the eggs and heavy whipping cream. Then, add the drained chopped spinach, shredded sharp Cheddar cheese, and diced yellow onion to the bowl.
2. Pour the mixture into a round baking dish and place it into the air fryer basket.
3. Adjust the temperature of the air fryer to 320ºF (160ºC) and bake for 20 minutes.
4. Once cooked, the eggs will be firm and slightly browned. Serve the pie immediately.

*Nutritional Information (Per Serving):*Calories: 263 / Fat: 20g / Protein: 18g / Carbs: 4g / Fiber: 1g / Sodium: 321mg

Cheesy Zucchini Boats

Prep time: 15 minutes / Cook time: 20 minutes
Serves 2

Ingredients:
• 2 medium zucchini
• 15ml (1 tablespoon) avocado oil
• 60ml (1/4 cup) low-carb, no-sugar-added pasta sauce
• 60g (1/4 cup) full-fat ricotta cheese
• 60g (1/4 cup) shredded Mozzarella cheese
• 1/4 teaspoon dried oregano
• 1/4 teaspoon garlic powder
• 1/2 teaspoon dried parsley
• 2 tablespoons grated vegetarian Parmesan cheese

Instructions:
1. Begin by preparing the zucchini. Cut off 1 inch from the top and bottom of each zucchini. Slice them in half lengthwise and use a spoon to scoop out a bit of the inside, creating room for the filling. Brush the zucchini with avocado oil and spoon 2 tablespoons of pasta sauce into each shell.
2. In a medium bowl, combine the ricotta cheese, shredded Mozzarella cheese, oregano, garlic powder, and parsley. Spoon the cheese mixture into each zucchini shell.
3. Place the stuffed zucchini shells into the air fryer basket and adjust the temperature to 350ºF (177ºC). Air fry for 20 minutes.
4. Once cooked, carefully remove the zucchini boats from the air fryer basket using tongs or a spatula. Sprinkle grated Parmesan cheese on top and serve immediately.

*Nutritional Information (Per Serving):*Calories: 208 / Fat: 14g / Protein: 12g / Carbs: 11g / Fiber: 3g / Sodium: 247mg

Broccoli Crust Pizza

Prep time: 15 minutes / Cook time: 12 minutes
Serves 4

Ingredients:
• 340g (3 cups) riced broccoli, steamed and well-drained
• 1 large egg
• 60g (1/2 cup) grated vegetarian Parmesan cheese
• 3 tablespoons low-carb Alfredo sauce
• 60g (1/2 cup) shredded Mozzarella cheese

Instructions:
1. In a large bowl, combine the riced broccoli, egg, and grated Parmesan checsc.
2. Cut a piece of parchment paper to fit the air fryer basket. Press the broccoli mixture onto the parchment paper to form a crust, dividing it into two batches if needed. Place the crust in the air fryer basket.
3. Adjust the temperature of the air fryer to 370ºF (188ºC) and air fry for 5 minutes.
4. Check if the crust is firm enough to flip. If not, air fry for an additional 2 minutes. Once firm, flip the crust.
5. Spread the Alfredo sauce over the crust and sprinkle the shredded Mozzarella cheese on top. Return the pizza to the air fryer basket and cook for an additional 7 minutes or until the cheese is golden and bubbling. Serve hot.

*Nutritional Information (Per Serving):*Calories: 87 / Fat: 2g / Protein: 11g / Carbs: 5g / Fiber: 1g / Sodium: 253mg

Air Fryer Cauliflower Steaks with Gremolata

Prep time: 15 minutes / Cook time: 25 minutes
Serves 4

Ingredients:
- 2 tablespoons olive oil
- 1 tablespoon Italian seasoning
- 1 large head cauliflower, outer leaves removed and sliced lengthwise through the core into thick "steaks"
- Salt and freshly ground black pepper, to taste
- ¼ cup Parmesan cheese

Gremolata:
- 1 bunch Italian parsley (about 1 cup packed)
- 2 cloves garlic
- Zest of 1 small lemon, plus 1 to 2 teaspoons lemon juice
- 120ml (½ cup) olive oil • Salt and pepper, to taste

Instructions:
1. Preheat your air fryer to 400ºF (204ºC).
2. In a small bowl, mix together the olive oil and Italian seasoning. Brush both sides of each cauliflower steak generously with the seasoned oil. Season with salt and black pepper to taste.
3. Arrange the cauliflower steaks in a single layer in the air fryer basket. If necessary, work in batches to ensure even cooking. Air fry for 15 to 20 minutes, turning the steaks halfway through cooking, until the cauliflower is tender and edges are golden brown.
4. Sprinkle Parmesan cheese over the cauliflower steaks and air fry for an additional 5 minutes.
5. To prepare the gremolata, in a food processor, combine the Italian parsley, garlic, lemon zest, and lemon juice. With the processor running, slowly add the olive oil until the mixture forms a bright green sauce. Season with salt and pepper to taste.
6. Serve the cauliflower steaks with the gremolata spooned over the top.

Nutritional Information (Per Serving):Calories: 336 / Fat: 30g / Protein: 7g / Carbs: 15g / Fiber: 5g / Sodium: 340mg

Air Fryer Crispy Tofu

Prep time: 30 minutes / Cook time: 15 to 20 minutes
Serves 4

Ingredients:
- 1 (16-ounce / 454-g) block extra-firm tofu
- 2 tablespoons coconut aminos
- 1 tablespoon toasted sesame oil
- 1 tablespoon olive oil
- 1 tablespoon chili-garlic sauce
- 1½ teaspoons black sesame seeds
- 1 scallion, thinly sliced

Instructions:
1. Begin by pressing the tofu for at least 15 minutes. Wrap it in paper towels and place a heavy pan on top to drain excess moisture.
2. After pressing, slice the tofu into bite-size cubes and transfer them to a bowl. Drizzle with coconut aminos, sesame oil, olive oil, and chili-garlic sauce. Cover and refrigerate for 1 hour or overnight.
3. Preheat your air fryer to 400ºF (204ºC).
4. Arrange the marinated tofu cubes in a single layer in the air fryer basket. Pause halfway through the cooking time to shake the basket for even cooking.
5. Air fry the tofu for 15 to 20 minutes until it becomes crispy.
6. Serve the crispy tofu with any accumulated juices from the air fryer, and garnish with black sesame seeds and thinly sliced scallions.

Nutritional Information (Per Serving):Calories: 173 / Fat: 14g / Protein: 12g / Carbs: 3g / Fiber: 1g / Sodium: 49mg

Air Fryer Cheese Stuffed Zucchini

Prep time: 20 minutes / Cook time: 8 minutes
Serves 4

Ingredients:

- 1 large zucchini (about 400g or 2 cups when cut into four pieces)
- 30ml (2 tablespoons) olive oil
- 240g (1 cup) Ricotta cheese, at room temperature
- 2 tablespoons chopped scallions
- 1 heaping tablespoon fresh parsley, roughly chopped
- 1 heaping tablespoon minced coriander
- 57g (2 ounces) Cheddar cheese, preferably freshly grated
- 1 teaspoon celery seeds
- ½ teaspoon salt
- ½ teaspoon garlic pepper

Instructions:

1. Place the zucchini pieces in the air fryer basket and cook at 350ºF (177ºC) for about 10 minutes. Check for doneness and cook for an additional 2-3 minutes if needed.
2. While the zucchini is cooking, prepare the stuffing mixture by combining Ricotta cheese, chopped scallions, parsley, coriander, Cheddar cheese, celery seeds, salt, and garlic pepper in a bowl.
3. Once the zucchini is cooked, carefully open them up. Divide the stuffing mixture evenly among the zucchini pieces.
4. Return the stuffed zucchini to the air fryer basket and cook for an additional 5 minutes.
5. Serve the cheese stuffed zucchini warm.

*Nutritional Information (Per Serving):*Calories: 242 / Fat: 20g / Protein: 12g / Carbs: 5g / Fiber: 1g / Sodium: 443mg

Air Fryer Pesto Vegetable Skewers

Prep time: 30 minutes / Cook time: 8 minutes /
Makes 8 skewers

Ingredients:

- 1 medium zucchini (about 200g), trimmed and cut into 1.25 cm (½ inch) slices
- 1 medium yellow onion (about 150g), peeled and cut into 2.5 cm (1-inch) squares
- 1 medium red bell pepper (about 150g), seeded and cut into 2.5 cm (1-inch) squares
- 16 whole cremini mushrooms (about 200g)
- 80ml (⅓ cup) basil pesto
- ½ teaspoon salt
- ¼ teaspoon ground black pepper

Instructions:

1. Prepare the vegetables by dividing the zucchini slices, onion, and bell pepper into eight equal portions. Thread each portion onto skewers, alternating with two mushrooms per skewer. Brush the skewers generously with basil pesto.
2. Season each skewer with salt and black pepper on all sides. Place the skewers into the air fryer basket, ensuring they are not overcrowded.
3. Adjust the air fryer temperature to 375ºF (191ºC) and air fry for 8 minutes, turning the skewers halfway through the cooking time.
4. Once done, the vegetables should be browned at the edges and tender-crisp. Serve the skewers warm.

*Nutritional Information (Per Serving):*Calories: 75 / Fat: 6g / Protein: 3g / Carbs: 4g / Fiber: 1g / Sodium: 243mg

Mediterranean Herb Tempeh

Prep time: 10 minutes + marinating time / Cook time: 15 minutes
Serves 4

Ingredients:
- 1 cup (about 250g) tempeh, pressed and cubed
- 1 tablespoon soy sauce
- 1/2 teaspoon smoked paprika
- 40g tomato paste
- 1 teaspoon garlic granules
- 1 tablespoon olive oil
- 1 tablespoon Mediterranean herb mix

Instructions:
1. Press the tempeh and cut it into cubes.
2. In a bowl, mix the tempeh with soy sauce, tomato paste, olive oil, smoked paprika, garlic granules, and Mediterranean herb mix until evenly coated. Allow it to marinate for 30 minutes.
3. Preheat the air fryer to 190°C (375°F).
4. Air fry the tempeh for 10 minutes, then flip and cook for an extra 5 minutes.
5. Serve and relish!

Nutritional Information (Per Serving): / Calories: 177 / Fat: 11g / Carbs: 7.8g / Fiber: 0.2g / Protein: 12.2g

Vegan Chicken

Prep time: 15 minutes / Cook time: 15 minutes
Serves 4

Ingredients:
- 1 cup (about 100g) dry soy chunks
- 1/4 cup (about 50g) plain flour
- 1 tsp garlic granules
- 1/2 tsp mustard powder
- 1 tsp Mediterranean mustard
- Sea salt and ground black pepper, to taste
- 1 tbsp olive oil

Instructions:
1. Begin by soaking the dry soy chunks in 200ml of boiling water for approximately 15 minutes. Once soaked, drain, rinse, and gently press out any excess water.
2. In a mixing bowl, combine the soaked soy chunks with plain flour, garlic granules, mustard powder, Mediterranean mustard, sea salt, and ground black pepper, ensuring all pieces are evenly coated.
3. Arrange the coated soy chunks in the lightly greased Air Fryer basket.
4. Preheat the Air Fryer to 180°C (350°F) and cook the vegan chicken for 15 minutes, remembering to flip them over halfway through to ensure even cooking.
5. Once cooked, serve and savor your delicious vegan chicken!

Nutritional Information (Per Serving): / Calories: 177 / Fat: 4.9g / Carbs: 26.1g / Fiber: 3.1g / Protein: 7.2g

Beet Falafel

Prep time: 10 minutes / Cook time: 22 minutes
Serves 4

Ingredients:
- 1 cup (200g) dried chickpeas, soaked overnight
- 1/3 cup (50g) chickpea flour
- 3/4 cup (100g) beets, peeled and grated
- 1 teaspoon baking powder
- 1 parsley sprig, chopped
- 1 medium onion, diced
- 2 garlic cloves, minced
- 1/2 tsp ground cumin
- 1 tsp dried coriander
- Sea salt and freshly ground black pepper, to taste
- 1 tbsp olive oil

Instructions:
1. Combine all ingredients thoroughly using a blender or food processor.
2. Form the mixture into bite-sized balls and gently flatten them with a fork.
3. Place the patties in the air fryer basket lightly coated with oil.
4. Air fry the falafel at 190°C (375°F) for approximately 22 minutes, making sure to shake the basket halfway through for even cooking.
5. Serve the falafel with pita bread and enjoy!

Nutritional Information (Per Serving): / Calories: 298 / Fat: 7.4g / Carbs: 44.5g / Fiber: 8.6g / Protein: 13.7g

Homemade Vegan Bean Burgers

Prep time: 10 minutes / Cook time: 20 minutes
Serves 4

Ingredients:
- 2 cups (300g) cooked and rinsed couscous
- 1 1/2 cups (300g) cooked or boiled red kidney beans, drained and rinsed
- 1 tbsp chia seeds
- 1 tbsp olive oil
- 1 small aubergine, trimmed and grated
- 2 garlic cloves, peeled
- 1 medium red onion, peeled and quartered
- Sea salt and cracked black pepper, to taste

Instructions:
1. In a blender or food processor, combine the couscous, red kidney beans, chia seeds, olive oil, grated aubergine, garlic cloves, red onion, sea salt, and cracked black pepper. Blend until well mixed.
2. Shape the mixture into burger patties and place them in the lightly oiled air fryer basket.
3. Cook the burgers in the air fryer at 185°C (365°F) for 20 minutes, flipping them over halfway through the cooking time.
4. Work in batches if needed to ensure even cooking.
5. Serve and enjoy!

Nutritional Information (Per Serving): / Calories: 273 / Fat: 5.5g / Carbs: 45.5g / Fiber: 10.1g / Protein: 11.4g

Air-Fried Asparagus and Mushrooms

Prep time: 10 minutes / Cook time: 8 minutes
Serves 2

Ingredients:
- 10.5 oz (300g) asparagus spears, trimmed
- 7 oz (200g) brown Italian mushrooms, halved
- 1 tbsp olive oil
- 1/2 tsp garlic powder
- 1 tsp cayenne pepper
- 1 tsp garlic granules
- Sea salt and freshly ground black pepper, to taste

Instructions:
1. In a bowl, toss the trimmed asparagus spears and halved brown Italian mushrooms with olive oil, garlic powder, cayenne pepper, garlic granules, sea salt, and freshly ground black pepper until evenly coated.
2. Place the seasoned asparagus spears and mushrooms in the lightly greased air fryer cooking basket.
3. Air fry them at 200°C (390°F) for 8 minutes, shaking the basket once or twice during the cooking time to ensure even cooking.
4. Once cooked, serve and enjoy!

Nutritional Information (Per Serving): / Calories: 120 / Fat: 7.2g / Carbs: 11.5g / Fiber: 4.1g / Protein: 6.2g

Caramelized Figs

Prep time: 10 minutes / Cook time: 15 minutes
Serves 4

Ingredients:
- 14 oz (400g) figs, halved
- 2 tbsp coconut oil
- 4 tbsp brown sugar
- 1 tbsp balsamic vinegar
- 1 tbsp lemon juice
- 1/4 tsp grated nutmeg
- 1/2 tsp ground cinnamon

Instructions:
1. In a bowl, toss the halved figs with coconut oil, brown sugar, balsamic vinegar, lemon juice, grated nutmeg, and ground cinnamon until well combined.
2. Place the fig halves in the air fryer cooking basket.
3. Air fry the figs at 170°C (340°F) for 15 minutes until they're caramelized.
4. Serve the caramelized figs with chilled Greek yogurt and honey.
5. Enjoy your delicious treat!

Nutritional Information (Per Serving): / Calories: 246 / Fat: 7.2g / Carbs: 48g / Fiber: 3.1g / Protein: 0.8g

Fig and Almond Crumble

**Prep time: 10 minutes / Cook time: 35 minutes
Serves 5**

Ingredients:
- 8.8 oz (250g) figs, pitted and halved
- Zest and juice of 1 small orange
- 2.1 oz (60g) clear Mediterranean honey
- Topping:
- 1 1/2 cups (150g) porridge oats
- 1/4 cup (50g) brown sugar
- 1/4 cup (50g) coconut oil, melted
- 3 tbsp (50ml) rum
- 1 tsp ground cinnamon
- 3.5 oz (100g) almonds, chopped

Instructions:
1. Toss the halved figs with orange zest, orange juice, and honey. Arrange them in a lightly greased baking tray.
2. In a mixing dish, thoroughly combine all the topping ingredients. Sprinkle the topping mixture over the layer of fruit.
3. Place the baking tray in the air fryer cooking basket.
4. Bake the crumble in the preheated Air Fryer at 165°C (330°F) for 35 minutes. Let it cool for 10 minutes before serving.
5. Enjoy your delicious Fig and Almond Crumble!

Nutritional Information (Per Serving): / Calories: 444 / Fat: 22.2g / Carbs: 56.2g / Fiber: 7.3g / Protein: 9.8g

Chapter 8: Grain and Legume Recipes

Barley and Bean Croquettes

Prep time: 10 minutes / Cook time: 18 minutes
Serves 4

Ingredients:
- 2 cups (400g) cooked barley, rinsed
- 1 cup (200g) cooked or boiled red kidney beans, drained and rinsed
- 1 tbsp olive oil
- 1 tsp Aleppo pepper
- 1 garlic clove, peeled
- 1 medium red onion, peeled and quartered
- 1 small carrot, trimmed and grated
- 7 oz (200g) cauliflower florets
- 1 medium egg
- Sea salt and cracked black pepper, to taste

Instructions:
1. In a blender or food processor, combine the cooked barley, red kidney beans, olive oil, Aleppo pepper, garlic clove, quartered red onion, grated carrot, cauliflower florets, egg, sea salt, and cracked black pepper.
2. Pulse the ingredients until well mixed.
3. Shape the mixture into balls and arrange them in the lightly oiled cooking basket of the air fryer.
4. Cook the croquettes in the air fryer at 185 degrees Celsius for 18 minutes, shaking the basket once or twice during cooking to ensure even browning.
5. Once cooked, serve the croquettes hot and enjoy!

Nutritional Information (Per Serving): Calories: 255 / Fat: 5.4g / Carbs: 44.1g / Fiber: 8.1g / Protein: 8.4g

Air Fryer Garlicky Bean Burgers with Sage

Prep time: 10 minutes / Cook time: 17 minutes
Serves 4

Ingredients:
- 4 cups (800g) cooked or boiled kidney beans, drained and rinsed
- 1 tbsp olive oil
- 1 bell pepper, deseeded and sliced
- 4 garlic cloves, peeled and halved
- 1 medium red onion, peeled and quartered
- 2 tbsp fresh sage
- Sea salt and cracked black pepper, to taste

Instructions:
1. In a blender or food processor, thoroughly combine the cooked kidney beans, olive oil, sliced bell pepper, halved garlic cloves, quartered red onion, fresh sage, sea salt, and cracked black pepper.
2. Pulse the ingredients until well mixed.
3. Shape the mixture into four burger patties and place them in the lightly oiled cooking basket of the air fryer.
4. Cook the burgers in the air fryer at 185 degrees Celsius for 17 minutes, turning them over halfway through the cooking time.
5. Once cooked, serve the bean burgers hot and enjoy!

Nutritional Information (Per Serving): Calories: 322 / Fat: 4.7g / Carbs: 53.3g / Fiber: 14.3g / Protein: 18.4g

Oat Muffins with Dried Figs

Prep time: 10 minutes / Cook time: 15 minutes
Serves 6

Ingredients:
- 2 medium ripe bananas
- 300g instant oats (3 cups)
- 100g dried figs, chopped (1 cup)
- 200ml almond milk
- 1 tbsp coconut oil
- 2 tbsp clear Mediterranean honey
- 1/2 tsp ground cinnamon
- 1 tsp ground cardamom
- A pinch of grated nutmeg
- A pinch of sea salt
- 1 tsp pure vanilla extract

Instructions:
1. In a mixing bowl, thoroughly combine the ripe bananas (mashed), instant oats, ground cinnamon, ground cardamom, grated nutmeg, sea salt, chopped dried figs, clear Mediterranean honey, coconut oil, and almond milk.
2. Spoon the mixture into lightly greased muffin cases.
3. Preheat the Air Fryer to 200 degrees Celsius.
4. Place the muffin cases in the preheated Air Fryer and bake the muffins for about 15 minutes.
5. Once baked, remove the muffins from the Air Fryer and allow them to cool slightly before serving.
6. Enjoy your delicious oat muffins with dried figs!

Nutritional Information (Per Serving): Calories: 336 / Fat: 7g / Carbs: 60.3g / Fiber: 8.3g / Protein: 10.5g

Air Fryer Fig and Goat Cheese Polenta Stacks

Prep time: 10 minutes / Cook time: 23 minutes
Serves 5

Ingredients:
- 600ml vegetable stock
- 120g quick-cook polenta (1 ½ cups)
- 1 tbsp butter, melted
- 1 tsp dried parsley flakes
- 1 tsp dried oregano
- 1 tsp chopped rosemary
- Sea salt and ground black pepper, to taste
- 8 medium figs, quartered
- 120g goat cheese, crumbled (1 ½ cups)

Instructions:
1. In a saucepan, bring the vegetable stock to a rapid boil, then reduce the heat to a gentle simmer.
2. Gradually stir in the polenta, melted butter, dried parsley flakes, dried oregano, chopped rosemary, sea salt, and black pepper. Stir continuously with a wire whisk for about 6 minutes until the polenta thickens.
3. Pour the cooked polenta into a baking tray and refrigerate until completely chilled.
4. Once chilled, cut the polenta into 9 squares using a sharp kitchen knife.
5. Preheat the Air Fryer to 190 degrees Celsius.
6. Place the polenta squares in the Air Fryer cooking basket and bake for about 17 minutes until they are golden and crispy.
7. Remove the polenta squares from the Air Fryer and top each square with quartered figs and crumbled goat cheese.
8. Serve hot and enjoy your delicious fig and goat cheese polenta stacks!

Nutritional Information (Per Serving): Calories: 299 / Fat: 13.2g / Carbs: 34.7g / Fiber: 4.3g / Protein: 13.1g

Air Fryer Energy Seed Bars

Prep time: 10 minutes / Cook time: 16 minutes
Serves 7

Ingredients:
- 200g sunflower seeds (1 cup)
- 200g pumpkin seeds (1 cup)
- 200g hemp seeds, hulled (1 cup)
- 200g oats (2 cups)
- 150g dried figs, chopped (1 cup)
- 150g almonds, slivered (1 cup)
- 80g coconut oil, softened (1/4 cup)
- 100g honey (1/2 cup)

Instructions:
1. In a mixing bowl, combine the sunflower seeds, pumpkin seeds, hemp seeds, oats, dried figs, slivered almonds, softened coconut oil, and honey.
2. Mix all the ingredients thoroughly until well combined.
3. Spoon the mixture into a parchment-lined roasting tin and press it down firmly with a wide spatula.
4. Preheat the Air Fryer to 180 degrees Celsius (356 degrees Fahrenheit).
5. Bake the mixture in the preheated Air Fryer for 16 minutes.
6. Allow it to cool completely before slicing it into bars.
7. Serve and enjoy your energy seed bars!

Nutritional Information (Per Serving): Calories: 399 / Fat: 20.2g / Carbs: 44.7g / Fiber: 8.1g / Protein: 13.4g

References

Broccoli Crust Pizza (Low-carb, Gluten free). (2016, April 21). Gimme Delicious. https://gimmedelicious.com/broccoli-crust-pizza-paleo-low-carb-gluten-free/

chicken. (n.d.). https://pixabay.com/photos/chicken-roasted-parchment-pepper-1081088/

Courtney. (2019, July 16). Black Bean and Corn Salsa. NeighborFood. https://neighborfoodblog.com/black-bean-and-corn-salsa/

Fotini. (2023, April 28). Feta Cheese Stuffed Zucchini. Real Greek Recipes. https://realgreekrecipes.com/cheese-stuffed-zucchini/

herbed mushrooms. (n.d.). https://pixabay.com/photos/mushrooms-vegetables-herbs-cooking-8058298/

Julia. (2018, February 26). Honey Lime Chicken Thighs. Julia's Album. https://juliasalbum.com/cilantro-lime-honey-chicken-thighs-recipe/

meatloaf. (n.d.). https://pixabay.com/photos/meal-meatloaf-flesh-food-cook-114297/

Mediterranean Pan Pizza - The California Wine Club - Recipes. (n.d.). Www.cawineclub.com. Retrieved March 16, 2024, from https://www.cawineclub.com/Mediterranean-Pan-Pizza_RP73.html

Muhammara (Mhammara Dip). (n.d.). Simply Lebanese. https://www.simplyleb.com/recipe/muhammara/

Quick-Braised Fresh Carrots and Sugar Snap Peas. (n.d.). The Spruce Eats. Retrieved March 16, 2024, from https://www.thespruceeats.com/braised-carrots-and-peas-4135663

ribs. (n.d.). https://pixabay.com/photos/flesh-ribs-meal-grilled-marinated-1613793/

Shrimp Pierogis w/ Sun-Dried Tomato Sauce. (n.d.). Good Food and Treasured Memories. Retrieved March 16, 2024, from https://goodfoodandtreasuredmemories.com/wp/recipe/shrimp-pierogis-w-sun-dried-tomato-sauce/

Unsplash. (2016, June 27). Photo by Casey Lee on Unsplash. Unsplash.com. https://unsplash.com/photos/cooked-food-awj7sRviVXo

Unsplash. (2017, December 22). Photo by Sameer Waskar on Unsplash. Unsplash.com. https://unsplash.com/photos/three-burgers-on-wooden-table-KojQfg8UdCE

Unsplash. (2018a, January 23). Photo by Mgg Vitchakorn on Unsplash. Unsplash.com. https://unsplash.com/photos/roasted-meat-served-on-ceramic-plate-Hs5gvdM8qo8

Unsplash. (2018b, January 30). Photo by Wine Dharma on Unsplash. Unsplash.com. https://unsplash.com/photos/fried-food-with-matcha-toppings-on-plate-LAQVVwmIZQI

Unsplash. (2018c, February 11). Photo by Kaitlyn Chow on Unsplash. Unsplash.com. https://unsplash.com/photos/grilled-patties-with-tomato-toppings-tIElrLKqdjo

Unsplash. (2018d, February 27). Photo by CA Creative on Unsplash. Unsplash.com. https://unsplash.com/photos/grilled-fish-cooked-vegetables-and-fork-on-plate-bpPTlXWTOvg

Unsplash. (2018e, April 21). Photo by Nick Fewings on Unsplash. Unsplash.com. https://unsplash.com/photos/baked-food-and-fried-potatoes-on-blue-plate-hfK401V_NXk

Unsplash. (2018f, June 15). Photo by Emiliano Vittoriosi on Unsplash. Unsplash.com. https://unsplash.com/photos/meat-balls-on-oval-white-plate-OFismyezPnY

Unsplash. (2018g, June 22). Photo by José Ignacio Pompé on Unsplash. Unsplash.com. https://unsplash.com/photos/person-slicing-juicy-medium-rare-meat-on-top-of-brown-wooden-cutting-board-XY-V_o-ykuk

Unsplash. (2018h, July 16). Photo by gladys arivia on Unsplash. Unsplash.com. https://unsplash.com/photos/fried-croqueta-on-chopping-board-wD0R5He4LtA

Unsplash. (2018i, August 22). Photo by charlesdeluvio on Unsplash. Unsplash.com. https://unsplash.com/photos/green-vegetable-plants-7OEiV-A8YwA

Unsplash. (2018j, December 5). Photo by Ksv Billi on Unsplash. Unsplash.com. https://unsplash.com/photos/meat-with-sauce-on-white-plate-7XYezj9RxYM

Unsplash. (2019a, February 3). Photo by sheri silver on Unsplash. Unsplash.com. https://unsplash.com/photos/baked-buns-on-round-wire-tray-Gwmz82WzD8w

Unsplash. (2019b, February 3). Photo by sheri silver on Unsplash. Unsplash.com. https://unsplash.com/photos/baked-buns-on-round-wire-tray-Gwmz82WzD8w

Unsplash. (2019c, February 17). Photo by Faisal on Unsplash. Unsplash.com. https://unsplash.com/photos/cooked-ribs-BS4Zeq7xDRk

Unsplash. (2019d, May 16). Photo by Emerson Vieira on Unsplash. Unsplash.com. https://unsplash.com/photos/person-cutting-meat-lanootd2FcU

Unsplash. (2019e, May 27). Photo by Roberto Carlos Román Don on Unsplash. Unsplash.com. https://unsplash.com/photos/cooked-food-in-bowl-AC6IAIhP4Yk

Unsplash. (2019f, August 7). Photo by Sergio Arze on Unsplash. Unsplash.com. https://unsplash.com/photos/plate-of-dessert-oeTdlanecpY

Unsplash. (2019g, December 11). Photo by Tengyart on Unsplash. Unsplash.com. https://unsplash.com/photos/egg-in-red-plastic-container-5G9qtofzT8s

Unsplash. (2020a, April 26). Photo by Anshu A on Unsplash. Unsplash.com. https://unsplash.com/photos/cooked-food-on-black-ceramic-plate-wmmLnCBcD-o

Unsplash. (2020b, April 26). Photo by Ulvi Safari on Unsplash. Unsplash.com. https://unsplash.com/photos/white-and-brown-pastry-with-strawberry-on-top-on-white-ceramic-plate-1rCjpJ6GFXw

Unsplash. (2020c, June 24). Photo by Sean Stone on Unsplash. Unsplash.com. https://unsplash.com/photos/cooked-meat-with-vegetable-on-white-ceramic-plate-0hOHNA3M6Ds

Unsplash. (2020d, July 1). Photo by Christian Coquet on Unsplash. Unsplash.com. https://unsplash.com/photos/brown-and-white-pastry-on-black-tray-p1sdDSn33Qc

Unsplash. (2020e, July 28). Photo by Mahmoud Fawzy on Unsplash. Unsplash.com. https://unsplash.com/photos/brown-bread-on-white-paper-jlTh4pmKxx0

Unsplash. (2020f, September 12). Photo by Mark König on Unsplash. Unsplash.com. https://unsplash.com/photos/fried-food-on-white-ceramic-plate-MyfbM2QYF4o

Unsplash. (2020g, September 26). Photo by Anshu A on Unsplash. Unsplash.com. https://unsplash.com/photos/brown-and-green-food-in-brown-plastic-container-iGkEDLE5-iQ

Unsplash. (2020h, October 5). Photo by Ryan Scott on Unsplash. Unsplash.com. https://unsplash.com/photos/brown-and-white-pizza-on-brown-wooden-table-YymkBdnHePg

Unsplash. (2020i, November 2). Photo by Farhad Ibrahimzade on Unsplash. Unsplash.com. https://unsplash.com/photos/green-vegetable-on-white-ceramic-bowl-30kYZsukwsk

Unsplash. (2020j, December 4). Photo by Max Griss on Unsplash. Unsplash.com. https://unsplash.com/photos/brown-bread-on-black-ceramic-plate-qbjkVIixPCY

Unsplash. (2020k, December 11). Photo by Jasmin Egger on Unsplash. Unsplash.com. https://unsplash.com/photos/white-egg-on-brown-wooden-tray-vWtfT-o-UOA

Unsplash. (2020l, December 15). Photo by Scott Eckersley on Unsplash. Unsplash.com. https://unsplash.com/photos/fried-chicken-on-black-plate-R-7_ErUOLxw

Unsplash. (2021a, January 3). Photo by Yuhan Du on Unsplash. Unsplash.com. https://unsplash.com/photos/sliced-meat-on-white-ceramic-plate-qsqVYKxqlzs

Unsplash. (2021b, January 7). Photo by Nathan Dumlao on Unsplash. Unsplash.com. https://unsplash.com/photos/cooked-food-on-white-ceramic-plate-8Uv6eanQWzY

Unsplash. (2021c, January 25). Photo by Davey Gravy on Unsplash. Unsplash.com. https://unsplash.com/photos/sliced-pizza-on-brown-wooden-chopping-board-d-tWHUbuEcY

Unsplash. (2021d, January 26). Photo by Davey Gravy on Unsplash. Unsplash.com. https://unsplash.com/photos/white-ceramic-plate-with-food-0YjyiBkNGdE

Unsplash. (2021e, February 21). Photo by camila waz on Unsplash. Unsplash.com. https://unsplash.com/photos/sliced-orange-fruits-on-brown-wooden-table-lUR7ZYeZSG8

Unsplash. (2021f, March 19). Photo by micheile henderson on Unsplash. Unsplash.com. https://

unsplash.com/photos/person-holding-stainless-steel-spoon-with-sliced-lemon-U71p52sAdOA

Unsplash. (2021g, April 23). Photo by D. L. Samuels on Unsplash. Unsplash.com. https://unsplash.com/photos/white-ceramic-plate-with-food-NYmm6gSD-cE

Unsplash. (2021h, July 18). Photo by Lucas Andrade on Unsplash. Unsplash.com. https://unsplash.com/photos/fried-chicken-on-stainless-steel-tray-3Uj0GwVmOeY

Unsplash. (2021i, August 14). Photo by Fernando Andrade on Unsplash. Unsplash.com. https://unsplash.com/photos/orange-clay-on-stainless-steel-fork-TrD7yA09Vg8

Unsplash. (2021j, November 28). Photo by Tyler Nix on Unsplash. Unsplash.com. https://unsplash.com/photos/a-woman-sitting-at-a-table-eating-a-piece-of-pizza-o56IekTS6TM

Unsplash. (2021k, December 2). Photo by Levi T. on Unsplash. Unsplash.com. https://unsplash.com/photos/a-piece-of-meat-with-sprinkles-on-it-CuhsuC_4vNU

Unsplash. (2022a, January 7). Photo by Dean Ricciardi on Unsplash. Unsplash.com. https://unsplash.com/photos/a-bowl-of-granola-with-a-spoon-in-it-FCR4UVfKGgw

Unsplash. (2022b, January 31). Photo by Thembi Johnson on Unsplash. Unsplash.com. https://unsplash.com/photos/a-cutting-board-topped-with-sliced-bell-peppers-eewm83mBW1E

Unsplash. (2022c, March 6). Photo by Samuel Agyeman-Duah on Unsplash. Unsplash.com. https://unsplash.com/photos/a-slice-of-quiche-on-a-white-plate-on-a-wooden-table-ivFdoHieX08

Unsplash. (2022d, August 16). Photo by Jessica Hearn on Unsplash. Unsplash.com. https://unsplash.com/photos/a-plate-of-food-2LXuRH4JCEM

Unsplash. (2022e, August 24). Photo by Getty Images on Unsplash. Unsplash.com. https://unsplash.com/photos/vegeterian-kitchen-beetroot-veggie-chips-and-guacamole-d4YJHt1vYzQ

Unsplash. (2022f, September 14). Photo by Getty Images on Unsplash. Unsplash.com. https://unsplash.com/photos/unrecognizable-man-washing-green-salad-leaves-in-the-kitchen-sink-2NumRaKwZPk

Unsplash. (2022g, September 27). Photo by Elena Leya on Unsplash. Unsplash.com. https://unsplash.com/photos/a-plate-of-food-7WBbsJqhTtQ

Unsplash. (2022h, October 3). Photo by Maryam Sicard on Unsplash. Unsplash.com. https://unsplash.com/photos/a-plate-of-cooked-cauliflower-with-a-side-of-ranch-dressing-14k6aNzMIeA

Unsplash. (2022i, October 3). Photo by Maryam Sicard on Unsplash. Unsplash.com. https://unsplash.com/photos/a-hamburger-sitting-on-top-of-a-wooden-cutting-board-2WvC5B16uRI

Unsplash. (2022j, October 3). Photo by Maryam Sicard on Unsplash. Unsplash.com. https://unsplash.com/photos/a-plate-of-tofu-next-to-a-bowl-of-rice-48UH8vTzVeI

Unsplash. (2022k, October 15). Photo by Jessica Tan on Unsplash. Unsplash.com. https://unsplash.com/photos/a-tray-of-food-NCNPlp7ZpKA

Unsplash. (2022l, November 17). Photo by Pablo Merchán Montes on Unsplash. Unsplash.com. https://unsplash.com/photos/a-plate-of-food-on-a-wooden-table-KlitNfI46kA

Unsplash. (2022m, December 7). Photo by Elena Leya on Unsplash. Unsplash.com. https://unsplash.com/photos/a-plate-of-food-DBVIb_rWUKw

Unsplash. (2023a, January 23). Photo by Anita Austvika on Unsplash. Unsplash.com. https://unsplash.com/photos/a-plate-of-mussels-on-a-table-with-a-bottle-of-wine-XFdtcySyLI0

Unsplash. (2023b, March 4). Photo by Natalia Gusakova on Unsplash. Unsplash.com. https://unsplash.com/photos/a-white-plate-topped-with-grilled-eggplant-and-potatoes-UdsV2iVWVOc

Unsplash. (2023c, March 13). Photo by Charlie Harris on Unsplash. Unsplash.com. https://unsplash.com/photos/a-person-dipping-a-tortilla-into-a-bowl-of-guacamole-7QlxhWr6SR4

Unsplash. (2023d, March 20). Photo by Anita Austvika on Unsplash. Unsplash.com. https://unsplash.com/photos/a-table-topped-with-plates-of-food-and-a-yellow-plate-z3K-ivnjY1Y

Unsplash. (2023e, April 24). Photo by Dan Dennis on Unsplash. Unsplash.com. https://unsplash.com/photos/a-tray-of-meat-and-potatoes-on-a-table-vre7ufv6ekE

Unsplash. (2023f, May 15). Photo by Elena Leya on Unsplash. Unsplash.com. https://unsplash.com/photos/a-bowl-of-chips-next-to-a-bowl-of-apples-31D8jOXzQQo

Unsplash. (2023g, August 18). Photo by Anna Jakutajc-Wojtalik on Unsplash. Unsplash.com. https://unsplash.com/photos/a-black-plate-topped-with-a-sandwich-and-cucumbers-_yM62g37WMg

Unsplash. (2023h, August 30). Photo by Diana Light on Unsplash. Unsplash.com. https://unsplash.com/photos/a-person-holding-a-wooden-cutting-board-with-different-types-of-food-on-it-lCOwqprXcwg

Unsplash. (2023i, August 30). Photo by Karolina Grabowska on Unsplash. Unsplash.com. https://unsplash.com/photos/a-wooden-table-topped-with-plates-of-food-bGEXLZTO1rQ

Unsplash. (2023j, September 25). Photo by Cristi Caval on Unsplash. Unsplash.com. https://unsplash.com/photos/a-wooden-cutting-board-topped-with-sliced-meat-ri74bNm-sHY

Unsplash. (2023k, September 27). Photo by Monika Grabkowska on Unsplash. Unsplash.com. https://unsplash.com/photos/a-couple-of-sandwiches-sitting-on-top-of-a-wooden-cutting-board-Gr9HnhcXslo

Unsplash. (2023l, October 14). Photo by rebootanika on Unsplash. Unsplash.com. https://unsplash.com/photos/a-white-plate-with-a-piece-of-cauliflower-on-it-SRHZA0Mf1V8

zucchini boats. (n.d.). https://pixabay.com/photos/zucchini-tomatoes-cheese-filled-1804460/

Traybake. (n.d.). https://www.pexels.com/photo/foods-on-a-tin-bowl-10050740/

Unsplash. (2017a, June 27). Photo by Toa Heftiba on Unsplash. Unsplash.com. https://unsplash.com/photos/vegetables-on-dish-beside-white-peony-flower-M0TpZ3yZh2Q

Unsplash. (2017b, September 12). Photo by Taylor Kiser on Unsplash. Unsplash.com. https://unsplash.com/photos/selective-focus-photography-of-muffin-on-top-of-table-zIR-P9dIGu8

Unsplash. (2017c, September 12). Photo by Taylor Kiser on Unsplash. Unsplash.com. https://unsplash.com/photos/stack-of-foods-beside-white-ceramic-bowl-iiQZcCtfpyk

Unsplash. (2017d, October 23). Photo by Allen Rad on Unsplash. Unsplash.com. https://unsplash.com/photos/three-pastries-on-ceramic-plate-with-fork-t7yR_y3IENE

Unsplash. (2018a, January 29). Photo by Joanna Kosinska on Unsplash. Unsplash.com. https://unsplash.com/photos/sliced-fruit-on-plate-beside-green-leaves-WgLYH-QEYT0

Unsplash. (2018b, April 30). Photo by Deryn Macey on Unsplash. Unsplash.com. https://unsplash.com/photos/shallow-focus-photo-of-hamburger-kPLccIMtS8E

Unsplash. (2018c, June 15). Photo by Jasmin Schreiber on Unsplash. Unsplash.com. https://unsplash.com/photos/selective-focus-photography-of-vegetable-salad-V2Kw-YC7Cls

Unsplash. (2019a, May 5). Photo by Diliara Garifullina on Unsplash. Unsplash.com. https://unsplash.com/photos/bowl-of-cooked-food-D5NFJDb9j8s

Unsplash. (2019b, July 3). Photo by Oklahoma Academy Country Store on Unsplash. Unsplash.com. https://unsplash.com/photos/green-vegetable-Hi6yn8RSD8Y

Unsplash. (2019c, October 14). Photo by Ilya Mashkov on Unsplash. Unsplash.com. https://unsplash.com/photos/meat-and-cheese-burger-surrounded-by-sesame-seeds-_qxbJUr9RqI

Unsplash. (2019d, November 5). Photo by Sujeeth Potla on Unsplash. Unsplash.com. https://unsplash.com/photos/green-vegetables-bSiO6a4rn0

Unsplash. (2020a, January 10). Photo by Fallon Michael on Unsplash. Unsplash.com. https://unsplash.com/photos/a-white-bowl-filled-with-granola-on-top-of-a-table-_d1K4GfapEk

Unsplash. (2020b, January 29). Photo by Sebastian Coman Photography on Unsplash. Unsplash.com. https://unsplash.com/photos/brown-bread-on-white-ceramic-plate-rtJCcnZgdRg

Unsplash. (2020c, April 4). Photo by micheile henderson on Unsplash. Unsplash.com. https://unsplash.com/photos/cooked-food-on-brown-wooden-tray-FQ1jwKG_q68

Unsplash. (2020d, May 14). Photo by Diliara Garifullina on Unsplash. Unsplash.com. https://unsplash.com/photos/white-ceramic-bowl-with-brown-rice-and-stainless-steel-spoon-RtB5Irx-H9c

Unsplash. (2020e, September 16). Photo by ABHISHEK HAJARE on Unsplash. Unsplash.com. https://unsplash.com/photos/vegetable-salad-in-black-bowl-EljLLnd7Mow

Unsplash. (2020f, September 16). Photo by engin akyurt on Unsplash. Unsplash.com. https://unsplash.com/photos/burger-on-white-ceramic-plate-BelVb9Fsc4U

Unsplash. (2020g, October 23). Photo by Priscilla Du Preez □□ on Unsplash. Unsplash.com. https://unsplash.com/photos/white-ceramic-bowl-on-brown-woven-basket-r8LxRcf7G3I

Unsplash. (2020h, November 9). Photo by Farhad Ibrahimzade on Unsplash. Unsplash.com. https://unsplash.com/photos/cooked-food-on-black-ceramic-bowl-KpOl9jV2aJM

Unsplash. (2020i, December 1). Photo by Prchi Palwe on Unsplash. Unsplash.com. https://unsplash.com/photos/cooked-food-on-white-ceramic-plate-3OMLWzkkt0Y

Unsplash. (2020j, December 4). Photo by Max Griss on Unsplash. Unsplash.com. https://unsplash.com/photos/brown-bread-on-black-ceramic-plate-qbjkVIixPCY

Unsplash. (2021a, February 27). Photo by Peter Pham on Unsplash. Unsplash.com. https://unsplash.com/photos/cooked-food-on-black-tray-v5yVy3IhSRU

Unsplash. (2021b, May 14). Photo by Adam Bartoszewicz on Unsplash. Unsplash.com. https://unsplash.com/photos/person-holding-burger-with-tomato-and-lettuce-ZWwgWqr_m28

Unsplash. (2021c, July 10). Photo by Farhad Ibrahimzade on Unsplash. Unsplash.com. https://unsplash.com/photos/vegetable-salad-on-brown-ceramic-bowl-beside-clear-wine-glass-zigoE-mFvKk

Unsplash. (2021d, November 25). Photo by Ludovic Avice on Unsplash. Unsplash.com. https://unsplash.com/photos/a-bowl-of-food-sitting-on-top-of-a-table-uIcLobU2sAU

Unsplash. (2021e, December 13). Photo by Angèle Kamp on Unsplash. Unsplash.com. https://unsplash.com/photos/a-table-topped-with-plates-and-bowls-of-food-raRH_DTQA3M

Unsplash. (2021f, December 22). Photo by Roberto Sorin on Unsplash. Unsplash.com. https://unsplash.com/photos/a-person-in-white-gloves-cutting-a-piece-of-cake-ZgL-jyqtcK4

Unsplash. (2022a, May 21). Photo by Kostiantyn Vierkieiev on Unsplash. Unsplash.com. https://unsplash.com/photos/a-white-plate-topped-with-sliced-up-vegetables-mKL-CLrUsB8

Unsplash. (2022b, October 3). Photo by Maryam Sicard on Unsplash. Unsplash.com. https://unsplash.com/photos/a-baking-tray-with-cookies-and-vegetables-on-it-aZcrQ06hxqI

Unsplash. (2022c, October 3). Photo by Maryam Sicard on Unsplash. Unsplash.com. https://unsplash.com/photos/a-white-plate-topped-with-food-next-to-a-pan-of-rice-k7-p6gy0rKI

Unsplash. (2022d, October 26). Photo by Jonathan Borba on Unsplash. Unsplash.com. https://unsplash.com/photos/a-pan-filled-with-green-beans-on-top-of-a-table-k4Q6MoolqVE

Unsplash. (2022e, November 7). Photo by Elena Leya on Unsplash. Unsplash.com. https://unsplash.com/photos/a-plate-of-food-0-mN0hGzqRQ

Unsplash. (2022f, November 25). Photo by Kawê Rodrigues on Unsplash. Unsplash.com. https://unsplash.com/photos/a-plate-of-shrimp-ntbqO-cCjIo

Unsplash. (2023a, January 23). Photo by Div Manickam on Unsplash. Unsplash.com. https://unsplash.com/photos/a-white-plate-topped-with-four-fried-food-items-la8l6y8_AHg

Unsplash. (2023b, July 29). Photo by Monika Grabkowska on Unsplash. Unsplash.com. https://unsplash.com/photos/a-salad-with-cucumbers-tomatoes-cucumbers-onions-cheese-d3vv-TeU9nk

Unsplash. (2023c, August 16). Photo by Monika Grabkowska on Unsplash. Unsplash.com. https://unsplash.com/photos/a-plate-of-food-on-a-pink-tiled-table-xBY6sFpWZjg

Unsplash. (2023d, August 30). Photo by Karolina Grabowska on Unsplash. Unsplash.com. https://unsplash.com/photos/a-wooden-table-topped-with-plates-of-food-bGEXLZTO1rQ

Unsplash. (2023e, October 12). Photo by Monika Grabkowska on Unsplash. Unsplash.com. https://unsplash.com/photos/a-white-plate-topped-with-food-next-to-a-glass-of-milk-cGhKKR0Cn8E

Unsplash. (2023f, November 20). Photo by Monika Grabkowska on Unsplash. Unsplash.com. https://unsplash.com/photos/a-casserole-dish-with-grapes-and-herbs-crrgfKFdBwg

INDEX

30-Day Meal Plan

	Breakfast	Lunch	Dinner	Snack/Dessert
Day 1	Homemade Gluten-Free Granola Cereal	Honey-Glazed Chicken Thighs	Short Ribs with Chimichurri	Lemon-Pepper Chicken Drumsticks
Day 2	Air Fryer Breakfast Hash	Air Fryer Pork Milanese	Zesty Lemon Mahi-Mahi	Mexican Potato Skins
Day 3	Air Fryer Butternut Squash and Ricotta Frittata	Roasted Cauliflower with Tahini Sauce	Pork Meatballs	Asian Five-Spice Wings
Day 4	Air Fryer Mini Shrimp Frittata	Turkey Tenderloin	Spiced Sweet Potato Cubes	Eggplant Fries
Day 5	Air Fryer Spinach and Mushroom Mini Quiche	Balsamic Tilapia	Cod and Potato Traybake	Lebanese Muhammara
Day 6	Air Fryer Italian Egg Cups	Buffalo Chicken Cheese Sticks	Air Fryer Kheema Meatloaf	Turkey Burger Sliders
Day 7	Air Fryer Mexican Breakfast Pepper Rings	Air Fryer Cube Steak Roll-Ups	Roasted Beets with Chermoula	Tex-Mex Style Tortilla Chips
Day 8	Air Fryer Veggie Frittata	Salmon and Cucumber Salad	Mediterranean Pan Pizza	Cinnamon-Apple Chips
Day 9	Air Fryer Smoky Sausage Patties	Cauliflower Pizza	Spicy Lamb Sirloin Chops	Shrimp Pirogues
Day 10	Air Fryer Spinach and Feta Egg Bake	Spicy Flounder Cutlets	Homemade Vegetable Burgers	Garlic-Roasted Mushrooms
Day 11	Air Fryer Jalapeño Popper Egg Cups	Chicken Lettuce Wraps	Garlic Rosemary Prawns	Curried Yogurt Greens Chips
Day 12	Air Fryer Buffalo Egg Cups	Air Fryer Baby Back Ribs	Homemade Pesto Spinach Flathread	Savory Black Bean Corn Dip
Day 13	Air Fryer Mexican Breakfast Pepper Rings	Parmesan-Coated Pork Cutlets	Everything Bagel Ahi Tuna Steaks	Mediterranean Herb Okra Chips
Day 14	Air Fryer Veggie Frittata	Chicken Patties	Crustless Spinach Cheese Pie	Roasted Beet Salad with Goat Cheese
Day 15	Air Fryer Smoky Sausage Patties	Spiced Salmon	Warm Sweet Potato Salad	Harissa Courgette and Corn Latkes

	Breakfast	**Lunch**	**Dinner**	**Snack/Dessert**
Day 16	Air Fryer Spinach and Feta Egg Bake	Cajun Blackened Pork Roast	Air Fryer Pork Rind Fried Chicken	Grilled Prawn Kabobs
Day 17	Air Fryer Jalapeño Popper Egg Cups	Tangy Beef Strips	Cheesy Zucchini Boats	Air Fryer Energy Seed Bars
Day 18	Air Fryer Buffalo Egg Cups	Air Fryer Cilantro Lime Chicken Thighs	Apple Cider Mussels	Air Fryer Fig and Goat Cheese Polenta Stacks
Day 19	Savoury Oats Greek Style	Crispy Shrimp Tacos	Air Fryer Cauliflower Steaks with Gremolata	Air Fryer Garlicky Bean Burgers with Sage
Day 20	Mediterranean Scrambled Eggs	Spicy Beef Shreds	Air Fryer Chicken Thighs with Cilantro	Barley and Bean Croquettes
Day 21	Tuna and Sweetcorn Fritters	Grilled Swordfish Skewers	Air Fryer Crispy Tofu	Lemon-Pepper Chicken Drumsticks
Day 22	Classic Savoury Muffins	Peppery Scallops	Air Fryer Garlicky Bean Burgers with Sage	Eggplant Fries
Day 23	Authentic Italian Frittata	Air Fryer Teriyaki Chicken Legs	Herb-infused Snapper En Papillote	Lebanese Muhammara
Day 24	Greek Breakfast Casserole	Herbed Mushroom Sirloin Bites	Air Fryer Pesto Vegetable Skewers	Tex-Mex Style Tortilla Chips
Day 25	Air Fryer Smoky Sausage Patties	Arugula, Chickpea, and Feta Salad	Crispy-Coated Catfish Delight	Mexican Potato Skins
Day 26	Air Fryer Italian Egg Cups	Mediterranean Herb Tempeh	Air Fryer Pecan Turkey Cutlets	Turkey Burger Sliders
Day 27	Air Fryer Breakfast Hash	Taco Chicken	Barley and Bean Croquettes	Cinnamon-Apple Chips
Day 28	Authentic Italian Frittata	Homemade Roasted Salsa	Chicken Gyros with Tzatziki Sauce	Curried Yogurt Greens Chips
Day 29	Air Fryer Mexican Breakfast Pepper Rings	Caramelized Figs	Chicken Mini Meatloaves	Savory Black Bean Corn Dip
Day 30	Homemade Gluten-Free Granola Cereal	Broccoli Crust Pizza	Speedy Shrimp Skewers	Shrimp Pirogues

MEASUREMENT CONVERSION CHART

VOLUME EQUIVALENTS(DRY)

US STANDARD	METRIC (APPROXIMATE)
1/8 teaspoon	0.5 mL
1/4 teaspoon	1 mL
1/2 teaspoon	2 mL
3/4 teaspoon	4 mL
1 teaspoon	5 mL
1 tablespoon	15 mL
1/4 cup	59 mL
1/2 cup	118 mL
3/4 cup	177 mL
1 cup	235 mL
2 cups	475 mL
3 cups	700 mL
4 cups	1 L

VOLUME EQUIVALENTS(LIQUID)

US STANDARD	US STANDARD (OUNCES)	METRIC (APPROXIMATE)
2 tablespoons	1 fl.oz.	30 mL
1/4 cup	2 fl.oz.	60 mL
1/2 cup	4 fl.oz.	120 mL
1 cup	8 fl.oz.	240 mL
1 1/2 cup	12 fl.oz.	355 mL
2 cups or 1 pint	16 fl.oz.	475 mL
4 cups or 1 quart	32 fl.oz.	1 L
1 gallon	128 fl.oz.	4 L

TEMPERATURES EQUIVALENTS

FAHRENHEIT(F)	CELSIUS(C) (APPROXIMATE)
225 °F	107 °C
250 °F	120 °C
275 °F	135 °C
300 °F	150 °C
325 °F	160 °C
350 °F	180 °C
375 °F	190 °C
400 °F	205 °C
425 °F	220 °C
450 °F	235 °C
475 °F	245 °C
500 °F	260 °C

WEIGHT EQUIVALENTS

US STANDARD	METRIC (APPROXIMATE)
1 ounce	28 g
2 ounces	57 g
5 ounces	142 g
10 ounces	284 g
15 ounces	425 g
16 ounces (1 pound)	455 g
1.5 pounds	680 g
2 pounds	907 g

The Dirty Dozen and Clean Fifteen

The Environmental Working Group (EWG) is a nonprofit, nonpartisan organization dedicated to protecting human health and the environment Its mission is to empower people to live healthier lives in a healthier environment. This organization publishes an annual list of the twelve kinds of produce, in sequence, that have the highest amount of pesticide residue-the Dirty Dozen-as well as a list of the fifteen kinds ofproduce that have the least amount of pesticide residue-the Clean Fifteen.

THE DIRTY DOZEN

- The 2016 Dirty Dozen includes the following produce. These are considered among the year's most important produce to buy organic:

Strawberries	Spinach
Apples	Tomatoes
Nectarines	Bell peppers
Peaches	Cherry tomatoes
Celery	Cucumbers
Grapes	Kale/collard greens
Cherries	Hot peppers

- *The Dirty Dozen list contains two additional itemskale/collard greens and hot peppers-because they tend to contain trace levels of highly hazardous pesticides.*

THE CLEAN FIFTEEN

- The least critical to buy organically are the Clean Fifteen list. The following are on the 2016 list:

Avocados	Papayas
Corn	Kiw
Pineapples	Eggplant
Cabbage	Honeydew
Sweet peas	Grapefruit
Onions	Cantaloupe
Asparagus	Cauliflower
Mangos	

- *Some of the sweet corn sold in the United States are made from genetically engineered (GE) seedstock. Buy organic varieties of these crops to avoid GE produce.*

Made in the USA
Las Vegas, NV
15 April 2024

80603517R00046